The Fenwick Lectures

The Fenwick Lectures

*Delivered at Fenwick University
in the Spring of 2019*

by John Panteleimon Manoussakis

Edited by Louis Light

Foreword by Matthew Clemente

SENEX
PRESS

To Anna, Felix, Griffin, Peter, Emmeline, McKenzie,
Michael, Andrew, and all the Young Fenwickians.

Then Adeimantus said, "Is it possible you don't know that at sunset there will be a torch race on horseback for the goddess?"

"On horseback?" I said. "That is novel. Will they hold torches and pass them to one another while racing the horses, or what do you mean?"

"That's it," said Polemarchus, "and, besides, they'll put on an all-night festival that will be worth seeing. We'll get up after dinner and go to see it; there we'll be together with many of the young men and we'll talk. So stay and do as I tell you."

Contents

The Infinite Leibniz

by Matthew Clemente

"Cunégonde is dead! Oh, best of all possible worlds, where are you?"

~Voltaire, *Candide, ou le Réalisme*

There was something uncanny—not to say *meta-real*—about receiving a draft of this work from the Editor-in-Chief of Senex Press along with an invitation to provide its foreword. In the first place that grammarian, a Ms. Jamieson de Quincey, is not unknown to me. As a bit of a cinephile, I am of course aware of the works of the late screenwriter Pablo Grisóstomo (1989-2011), and so recognized immediately what I can only take to be the real world visage that inspired the creation of his most infamous character, the anti-heroine whose misadventures we follow in the ominously titled, and tragically still unproduced, <u>Murder as a Work of Art</u>. But beyond that, I felt a strange admixture of honor and angst at being entrusted with the profound responsibility of offering the first word to this, Manoussakis's last. As the reader is no doubt aware, Fr. John Panteleimon Manoussakis lived as a recluse for more than seven years. Indeed, over that span, I had been one of the few persons permitted to see him, and always at nighttime when the cloud of darkness veils the earth, obscuring what is seen and leaving one with questions, if not doubts, about one's senses. Our visits always seemed to me to be teeming with meaning, as if some infinite joy was about to burst forth and overflow.

What was it that we shared at those late hours that had us laughing like schoolboys? That, dear reader, I will not disclose. Some things are best kept in the shadows. I will, however, tell you the true story of our friendship, how it began, what it has meant to me, and how it changed after that fateful day in February of 2019 when Fr. Manoussakis mysteriously disappeared from this world only to reemerge a short time later utterly transformed, a new creation for whom all things had been made new. Venture with me, then, into the past. Let us turn the clock back some twenty years to the fall of 2007 when I was a bit rounder than I am today and every bit as conceited.

It was, if memory holds, the first day of my freshman year, and I was on my way from my dormitory, Mulledy Hall, to the academic building named, perhaps prophetically, for the Catholic convert and phenomenologist Edith Stein. I had stopped, as would become my custom, to get myself an iced coffee with two Splendas and was cutting through Fenwick Hall when I noticed a young, greasy-haired professor with a thick black beard walking in front of me. I was struck by him immediately, first, because he was wearing a bowtie which seemed utterly ridiculous—as if he wanted too badly to be Jean-Luc Marion but was instead some sort of Greek parody of Jean-Luc Beauchard who has been known to sport such attire purely in jest—and second because there was something unreal about his entire demeanor. He looked, it seems to me thinking back now, like one who has read too many Russian novels and decided on a whim to commit himself to pretending, for the rest of his life, that he was in one.

This fool, I thought, *cannot possibly teach here*—not knowing that that descriptor, *fool*, would one day be appended to his name by the cult of followers who in recent years have called for the canonization of their beloved St. JPM, Fool of the Most High.

As I emerged from Fenwick on the other side of the building, where G. K. Chesterton once planted a crab tree, I realized that I was following this strange man as if he were leading me, like some pied piper of old, wherever he wanted to go. Indeed, we continued on the same course, him but a few paces ahead of me, all the way to the stairs that descended down to the academic building. It was there, as we approached Stein Hall together, that something extraordinary happened. This saintly monk, this charming Greek philosopher, walked through the open doors—and let them shut in my face. Was this some sort of symbolic gesture? Was he, perhaps, attempting to teach me—here, on the threshold on my first philosophy class—that the true lover of wisdom must humble himself and learn to enter not by the main gate but through the narrow pass? No, as I would come to discover only moments later, he was just a prick. For, upon opening the door for myself and making my way to his classroom, I was greeted by this young academician—a newly minted PhD whose condescension, at that time, seemed wholly unmerited—with an arched eyebrow and bemused grin as he muttered under his breath, yet loud enough for the entire class to hear: "Sweatpants and a hoody? Angels and ministers of grace defend us! They dress as if they've just rolled out of bed on this campus!"

Appearance, I soon learned, was a significant preoccupation of the young Manoussakis's. For, although he was younger then than I am now and far less accomplished—he was merely a Visiting Professor at the time and not the Director of an important Center like me!—he nevertheless carried himself with the air of one whose academic achievements merited admiration. And admire him I did, not knowing then that, brilliant as he was, his true brilliance was hidden like a lamp under a bushel and would not shine forth until that magical visit to Fenwick University some twelve years later. But more on that in the pages to come. What I want to note now is that I can still fully recollect that initial lecture—the first he gave at the College of the Holy Cross and the first I attended as an undergraduate. It was on the uselessness of philosophy, the value we give to that which is useless, how resisting utility can have a humanizing effect. Those who have read my work well—and I imagine that anyone picking up this volume has been compelled to do so because he's seen that I have graced it with this Foreword, what other reason could he have for condescending to buy it?—those, I say, who are well acquainted with my writing will recognize the influence that that first lecture has had on my thinking ever since. Indeed, my recent writing on *metarealism* would be impossible without it.

In any event, I was impressed with Manoussakis and desired to know him better. Perhaps, I thought, if I spent enough time with him, he might be so good as to rub some of his genius off on me. And so, I started walking with him to and from class, making sure to open wide the door before him as he had refused, at least initially, to do for me. I would frequent his office hours, iced coffee in hand, and listen as he waxed poetic on topics ranging from the poetry of Joseph Crabtree to the formation of the blastopore in the early stages of embryonic development to the pronunciation of the letter H (*aitch* or *haitch*) as a shibboleth used in Northern Ireland to distinguish Catholics from heretics to the plays of Aristophanes, the superiority of *The Clouds* to *The Birds*, to the veneration of animals as folk saints and his anticipated canonization of Diego, his pet cat. We began meeting for dinners in Boston and even founded our own secret society, *The*

Society of the Flying Inn, which, come to think of it, was an obvious precursor to . . . well, never you mind that—

The years went by and I advanced in my studies, schooling myself at the feet of such masters as Jameson, Daniels, Beam, Cuervo, and of course, the inimitable Dr. McGillicuddy. But none taught me more than Manoussakis, a man whose intellect was larger and wit more piercing than any book I have ever read. If I have, to this point, made the Greek sound—*je ne sais pas*—affected, if I've implied that his pretense came off as a bit too pretension, that is because he was and it did. But to his immense credit, Manoussakis was never dull. No, anything but. There was, rather, a sort of fascination that affixed itself to him and had the uncanny effect of making him more attractive the more he lived into his part. To me, he was at once a Zosima and an Ivan, alternating between the sinner and the sage, today, an image of the beatific vision, tomorrow, the *via negative* personified. Sometimes, we'd go out and have a romping good time, bursting with laughter and drunken—not to say *debauched*—humor. At his merriest, there was no one who rivaled Manoussakis in his merriment. But at his lowest, when caught in the grips of his own personal dark night of the soul—well, few have descended lower, few feasted more bitterly on the foul entrails of despair. I will not dwell here—for, I have always agreed with Kierkegaard that *dvæle er djævelen*—but I will say that at some moments, my relationship with the good priest made me grateful for the doctrine of the Harrowing of Hell.

Manoussakis was, this is to say, an infinite and all-various man. Much like me, he had a knack for inhabiting different characters and bringing them to life. Yet unlike me, whose multiplicity is merely a fancy of the mind, Manoussakis specialized in inventing and reinventing himself. He was a multitude of his own, a man whose depths could not be plumbed, whose heights reached up and touched the clouds. And this was all before he ever set foot on the campus of Fenwick University. That hallowed institution was, of course, legendary in its time. But due to the unfortunate mismanagement of its immediate past president—a man whose name has become so notorious that I need not mention it here—it had, by the winter of 2019, fallen from the cultural imaginary and been nearly forgotten. Still, with the exception of a few lackluster adjuncts—hired, I'm told to proctor the courses its world-class faculty were too busy thinking to teach—Fenwick nevertheless remained one of the last bastions carrying forth the mantle of the great American intellectual tradition that prioritizes character over commerce and novel thought over thoughtless novelty.

It was, therefore, the ideal place for Manoussakis to undergo what can only be described as his conversion. Like Paul being bucked from his horse, like Augustine butchering the words of Paul and Beauchard misreading Augustine,[1] the Greek was changed all at once and infinitely for the better. Finally freed from playing a part, he became who he had always been, an utterly unique creation, a man of marvelous character, noble, charming, and true. Indeed, in reading through the lectures appended to this Foreword, I cannot help but reflect on the truth they convey. Not only is there wisdom in Manoussakis's words, and thus philosophical truth, not only can I attest to the veracity of this document as a historical record,

---

1   See, "The rest of the story [of my conversion] can be guessed by anyone with an ounce of knowledge of the Catholic intellectual tradition. I read Augustine and was profoundly changed. I found in his writings the room I needed to be wayward, to experience the pangs of uncertainty and even doubt." Stojkovich, "Serious Play: An Interview with Jean-Luc Beauchard" in *The Montreal Review* (January 2024).

and thus it is factually true, I am impressed by how true to life is the Manoussakis of page. Knowing him as I did after he returned from his sojourn to Fenwick, I can say with absolute honesty that this book has captured the man and contains his personality with such astonishing authenticity that it is really him you meet within. Here he is, preserved forever, in the finest of all possible worlds, strolling through the campus of his beloved Fenwick University, giving lectures, raising toasts, and exchanging barbs and witticisms with such noble personages as Sir Richmond Rugg, Dr. Simon Flaxmore, and, of course, the ingenious Professor Pangloss.

Indeed, if the man who preserved this work, Louis Light, was as clever as he fashions himself to be, he would no doubt have recognized that not only are *The Fenwick Lectures* arranged in Manoussakis's signature tripartite structure, they also mark the successful completion of his intellectual trilogy organized around the Transcendentals: the Good (*The Ethics of Time*), the Beautiful (*God After Metaphysics*), and now the True (*The Fenwick Lectures*). For below you will find the most truthful book ever written, excepting perhaps one—and that one was not written by man, though it did, without question, inspire the man—sacred, wonderful, and pleasing—whom you are about to meet in the pages below.

MSC

February 8th, 2026

The Conversion of Manoussakis, Fool of the Most High

Editor's Prefatory Note

In preparing the manuscript of this book for publication, I have consulted the original notes of Manoussakis's lectures, kept in folio 6729/19 of the Fenwick Archives (see the Appendix for autographic samples). That these lectures have remained unsurpassable in content as well as in form must be attributed to their long period of maturation. Manoussakis wrote them very slowly, adding a sentence here and a citation there over a period of several years, like a man slow-cooking a soup to which he adds ingredients with each reheating so that, by the end, his work approximates that process of chemical reduction that we associate more with alchemy than with cooking, and even less so with writing.

Of the four lectures originally scheduled and announced, we have only the first three. As the reader will discover, the final lecture was never delivered. With the fourth and final lecture missing, Manoussakis's Fenwick tetralogy remains an unfinished play in three acts—mirroring, perhaps, that tetralogy of Platonic dialogues which now includes only the *Republic*, the *Timaeus*, and the *Critias* (three dialogues that, interestingly enough, also take place during four consecutive days), the missing fourth being the *Hermocrates* (or, as some have speculated, the *Momucles*). Perhaps in recognition of that fact, Beauchard, a Roman priest (who was in attendance at the momentous occasion of the delivery of these lectures and, as the reader shall discover in the pages to follow, played an active role in that event), supplanted what the Byzantine monk could not accomplish by writing what became *City of Man: A Novel Reading of Plato's Republic* (Cascade, 2023), to which Manoussakis has appended his unqualified endorsement.

In any case, there is as little doubt about the originality of these lectures as there is of their authenticity. For by being *three* lectures, of which the second is further divided into *three* sections, they bear the unmistakable mark of Manoussakis's signature tripartite structure that organizes his previous major monographs—namely, the three senses (seeing, hearing, and touching) he uses to divide *God After Metaphysics* and the three gardens around which he organizes *The Ethics of Time*. In *The Fenwick Lectures* the triadic scheme takes the form of the three consecutive days over the course of which the lectures themselves were delivered. As if to hide the secret of their structure in the middle of the text, Manoussakis divides the second lecture into a further three sections corresponding to the canonical hours of the day (the *Terce*, the *Sext*, and the *None*). Since at the beginning of the *Sext*, he has appended an epigram suggesting that the material at that time has something to do with the Fall of Man, and further, as an epigram on top of the *None* suggests, since the material of the third station has something to do with the Last Judgement, we can justly assume that the first section of this lecture, namely the *Terce*, is about Creation. The association is not difficult to see; in fact, it is hard to miss. It would, thus, seem that the centerpiece of *The Fenwick Lectures* is meant to reflect a rather ambitious and daring plan that encompasses the entire span of the human drama, from its origins to its eschatological destiny—thus fulfilling the promise that Manoussakis made to his audience, that is, to provide a sort of (very short) *commedia umana*. If my interpretation is correct, then, *The Fenwick Lectures* takes the form of something comparable to a medieval altarpiece, with each of its three lectures representing a different panel in the Fenwick triptych.

The success of *The Fenwick Lectures*—which has carried its faithful devotees to extremes, as in the remarkable case of the Lithuanian composer who went so far as to attempt (and fail) to turn this work into the libretto for an opera—depends not so much on its structure, or the odd sequence of events that occasioned its writing, but rather Manoussakis's greatest creation: that is, the lecturer with whom he identifies and whose brilliant voice we hear in its adapted grand style unfolding page after page. After a little while we come to realize that we have been paying less attention to what is *said* and more to him who is saying it. Behind his semi-biographical digressions, his peculiar turn of phrase, his longwinded citations, his odd associations of ideas, his eclectic choice of references, the features of a strange character begin to emerge—if only in outline. To the extent, however, that Manoussakis the author does not coincide with Manoussakis the character, the latter appears as an exaggerated caricature, as if Manoussakis were attempting to fake his own accent, and the whole affair is, at the end, saved by self-parody.

Generations of Fenwick students have been introduced to philosophy by means of these lectures, since Fenwick University made of them a required course for all its freshmen—naming it "The Castelli Seminar" after the Castelli Hill, the only elevation in the lecturer's home village of Eretria, which he frequently climbed in order to escape the boredom of his childhood. Since the author in his Prologue provides a detailed account of the occasion of his visit to Fenwick University and the circumstances under which *The Fenwick Lectures* were delivered, it is unnecessary for me to do so and I can, therefore, relieve myself of that task. Finally, the initials of the editor's name within square brackets [L.L.] at the beginning of a note indicates that the note belongs to the editor and him alone.

Louis Light
Master of the Vault & Keeper of Secrets
Fenwick University
January 14, 2026
The Feast of the Ass

The Author's Prologue

"You have degraded what should have been a course of lectures into a series of tales."

~ Sherlock Holmes,
"The Adventure of the Copper Beeches"

A tale needs to be told and—believe me, good reader, no matter how extraordinary it might seem, for it is indeed extraordinary—it is, in Lucian's words, *a true story*; for, it tells the truth (the whole truth and nothing but the truth) of what happened that cold Friday morning while I was on my way to class. February 8, 2019 was one of those cold and dreary winter days in New England when everything around you is grey and brown, so it is all the more remarkable that such a dreary day became the *Vorspiel* to the colorful drama that unfolds in four acts through these Fenwick Lectures. It is, therefore, indispensable that the reader be told of the singular events that transpired while I was about to cross the campus of the College of the Holy Cross in Worcester, Massachusetts.

First, a few words are in order with regards to the topology of this campus; for the good reader will fail to follow the description of the extraordinary circumstances that gave birth to the lectures he is about to read without some rudimentary familiarity with that little corner of our college that became the scene of the impending drama. Thankfully no cartographer needs to be employed, for all the reader has to imagine is a triangle [ABC] with each of its two sides [AB and AC] emanating from one common point, Dinand Library, and extending—one [AB], toward Smith Hall, where my office was located, and the other [AC], toward Stein Hall, where my class was held. The hypotenuse [BC] of our topographical triangle, then, was the precise path that I was about to trace, as I had done so many times before on the way from my office to the classroom when, on that particular morning, I was suddenly intercepted, and all but kidnapped, by the emissaries of Fenwick University.

If I have learned one thing after all the years that I have had the privilege of teaching at the College of the Holy Cross, it is that the best way to go to class is by crossing the Memorial Plaza and, by cutting through Fenwick Hall, to emerge on the other side of the building, where G. K. Chesterton once planted a tree. I was just about to take that shortcut through Fenwick when I was stopped by five representatives of Fenwick University.[2] Let me immediately clarify, so as to avoid any confusion, that the two names have nothing in common: Fenwick University receives its dignified name *not* from Benedict Fenwick (bishop of Boston, founder of the College of Holy Cross, and namesake of Fenwick Hall), but rather from *John* Fenwick: "one of five Jesuits caught in the web of lies concocted by Titus Oates who accused the Jesuits of plotting to assassinate King Charles III and overthrow the government."[3]

---

2   I remember saying, "The embassy to Achilles had only three men—if it wasn't for that dual in Book IX that proves that there was a Homer who also knew how to write—and Fenwick University sends to me no less than five?" It was upon this point that they praised me as being "the one and only real Greek," on which see below. In response to my question, one said: "Our strength is not in numbers."

3   See, the Society of Jesus' official website under "Blessed John Fenwick." I cannot resist citing the following words from this entry: "Although the story was patently fictitious, the Jesuits paid with their lives."

I was about to cross Fenwick Hall on my way to class to teach Plato when a number of my audience (you are now my friends, gentlemen, and there can be no objection to my telling you this)—intercepted me and introduced themselves as emissaries sent by Fenwick University to bestow upon me the honor of delivering the four lectures named after the priest who was falsely accused and executed. The honor was extraordinary and came accompanied with such laudatory exclamations that I was reduced to blushing at the discrepancy between the praise and the thing praised, though I came very near to believing them when they called me "the one and only real Greek," and such nonsense.[4] The semester before I had completed my seminar on Plato, the transcript of which was praised by no less an authority of all things Greek than

---

4   The episode of February 8, 2019 is so uncannily similar to the episode of February 8, 169 AD, that Lucian narrates, in a rare autobiographical note, at the beginning of his essay on Zeuxis (see, Loeb's edition of Lucian's works, volume VI, pp. 154-157) that I request the reader's understanding if I don't waste time and effort in trying to come up with my own words to say what happened to me when I can just quote what happened to him without sacrificing a bit from the accuracy of my story. For the sake of the accuracy of *his* story, however, I quote here Chapman's superior translation of this passage (from his *Lucian, Plato and Greek Morals*, [Boston: Houghton Mifflin Company, 1931, pp. 19-21]): "I was lately walking home after lecturing when a number of my audience (you are now my friends, gentlemen, and there can be no objection to my telling you this)—these persons, then, came to me and introduced themselves, with the air of admiring hearers. They accompanied me a considerable way, with such laudatory exclamations that I was reduced to blushing at the discrepancy between the praise and the thing praised. Their chief point, which they were absolutely unanimous in emphasizing, was that the substance of my work was so fresh, so crammed with novelty. (...) Why, I have been absurdly self-satisfied, and come very near believing them when they called me the only and only real Greek, and such nonsense."

Sir Richmond Rugg. It was the reputation of my reading of Plato offered in that seminar that prompted Sir Rugg to nominate me for the Fenwick Lectures.

I knew, of course, of the Fenwick Lectures; they are legendary among academic circles. For the names of past speakers in that *libro d'oro* rang as if they were themselves made of gold: the English poet Joseph Crabtree (who came to Fenwick University accompanied by a young Edgar Allan Poe, whom the English poet, known for his fondness for refined spirits, had met in New Orleans), the American psychologist William James (accompanied by S. Freud, who had received a doctorate from Clark), the aforementioned G. K. Chesterton (in 1930)[5] and, more recently, Professor Simon Flaxmore of Oxford University—a genuine classicist if ever there was one. Who was I, even if I were to believe that I was in Lucian's words, "the one and only real Greek," to stand next to such illustrious names?

Besides the unsurpassed honor that they bestowed immediately and perpetually upon the fortunate academic who is nominated and so ennobled as the Fenwick lecturer-to-be (something that, undoubtedly, he dreamt since his boyhood, though remaining prudently reticent about it in public), the Fenwick Lectures are widely known for the unorthodox way by which the nominees are summoned. You see, there is *no* proper notification, nor even as much as an invitation, but rather the chosen academic is called to the task—which is also a trial and a test—*suddenly.* In most such endowed lectureships, an evaluation of the qualifying applicants typically *precedes* the process of nomination and selection; in the case of the Fenwick Lectures, however, the lectures themselves are

---

5   This visit has been well-documented in the electronic version of Fenwick University's archives.

the test and contest by which the chosen candidate is to prove whether he deserves to be remembered or—should he fail to rise to the occasion—have his name stricken from the annals of history. The reason for this is the belief that only the scholar who, while caught completely unawares and unprepared, is still capable of delivering a four-day long discourse on first philosophy, should be bestowed the honor of having his *extempore* lectures transcribed and transmitted by the University's Keeper of Secrets and thus immortalized by Senex Press, Fenwick University's Publication House and sole proprietor of the publication rights to—in descending order of importance—the Fenwick Lectures, the Fenwick Theses[6], the Fenwick Commentaries, and the Fenwick Notes (including the Fenwick Footnotes).

And yet, this is not all that was odd about my visitors and the conditions of their offer. I was to follow them— they *insisted*—to Fenwick University at once, with no time to notify my students of my hurried departure or my colleagues of the unexpected honor;[7] and I was to be taken there—hard as it is to believe—through the men's restroom that is located on the ground level of Fenwick Hall. It was perhaps this unceremonious entrance to Fenwick University that inspired in me the scatological theme of *inter faeces et urinam nascimur* that was to be developed at length in my first lecture. To my surprise, inside the men's restroom there is, indeed, a small door that hides

---

6   Among these, the first is an essay that claims Cervantes was the most important philosopher of the first Christian millennium; while the second hails Plato as the greatest novelist of pagan antiquity.

7   A week later, however, a headline published in one of the College's student newspapers read: "Professor Manoussakis of Philosophy Dept. on Unexpected Leave" (*The Spire*; February 15, 2019). <https://hcspire.com/2019/02/15/professor-manoussakis-on-unexpected-leave/>

the narrow entrance to an underground passage. In all my years using this restroom myself, I had never noticed it before. That passage leads under and beyond the campus to an abandoned train station over the Blackstone canal (which, from what I could judge based on my familiarity with Worcester's railroads, was neither part of the Commuter rail nor of the CSX railways).

"I detect that a train has been through here," I observed, for philosophical detection has always been my *forte*. "I can clearly see its tracks."

Indeed, a train-wagon that looked as if it had escaped from a French novel soon arrived, and by the intermittent fits of an asthmatic locomotive, we were slowly transported from Holy Cross to the gates of Fenwick University.

The campus of Fenwick University—so beautiful in its situation, so lofty, so majestic the appearance of it—left me standing there for a few minutes rapt in contemplation of how ironic and contrary to my expectations it was that as noble a place as *this* was to be reached through as ignominious a means as a college bathroom! Pen, my dear reader, can but ill describe it, the pencil not much better; for this is a place only fit to be talked of upon the very spot, when its buildings are under view, to be considered in all its aspects. Knowing fully well my limitations, therefore, I shall not attempt to describe it, as any attempt at description is destined to fail, except, perhaps, to say that the Philosophy Department of Fenwick University was housed in a large Edwardian building to which my five companions directed me, still dazed and confused by the unreality of the whole affair.

After a short tour around the campus, we entered the hall and saw in front of us a room packed with scholars and scholastics. Among the first, was of course, the President of Fenwick University, Dr. Anthony Joseph, seated in the very front of the room on a leather armchair.

Next to him, I recognized the young and up-and-coming Jefferey Burnop and behind him, the more senior members of Fenwick's faculty, such as Sir Richmond Rugg and Fr. Beauchard. There was also Dr. Damaris Tighe and a man who, from where I was standing, looked very much like Prof. Denys Turner of Yale University. It is possible, of course, that I was mistaken and he was someone who only looked like the renowned Professor, a pseudo-Denys, so to speak, or rather a pseudo-Turner. All the Young Fenwickians were in attendance, and, in the back galleries, one could see even a few of the brothers from the Brotherhood of the Thyrsus.

Without wasting any more time, I mounted the wooden platform and, standing behind the lectern, addressed my impatient audience thus—

My Young Fenwickians,

As I was walking through your beautiful campus, admiring its great buildings, I noticed that there is an inscription over the main entrance of your Philosophy Hall that reads,

Quid est Homo, quod Memor es ejus?

It is a question that I recognize as taken from Psalm 8 verse 4 translated, in your King James Bibles, as:

"What is man that thou art mindful of him?"

What is man?

In response to this question, I propose, in this series of lectures with which Fenwick University has honored me, to pursue a fourfold inquiry into this very question that you have thoughtfully inscribed over your heads: "What is Man that [God] is mindful of him?"[8] My answer will present you with a drama in four acts (a *Commedia Umana* perhaps), each underscoring a particular aspect of the being that we ourselves are:

Act I: *From Womb to Tomb*, in which we will consider human mortality and mechanical immortality, posthumous life and exhumed wealth or the plutocracy of the Underworld;

Act II: *The Rise of Anthropos*, in which orthograde bipedalism and the origins of techno-logy and con-science will be taken under our consideration;

---

8   Not only this, but also "What sort of Man is capable of thinking of God?" or rather, as we shall find out in the course of these lectures, "What sort of men are those who are *not* capable of thinking of God, and when, on those rare occasions they do, what sort of idols do their gods turn out to be? A variant of the Vulgate preserves a different reading of this verse: *Quid est Homo, quod Memnon est?* ("Who is the Man that is Memnon?") But I can't entertain such a reading seriously here.

Act III: *Persona/Prosopon*, that is, an examination into Man as a personal being and the origins of community; and, finally,

Act IV: *From the City-Soul to the City-State*, in which Man is examined as a political being and as a citizen of civilization.

The First Day

From Womb to Tomb

1. Of the Origins of Man

If our drama begins with the *human* and from the soil, that is because our word "human" comes from the Latin *humus*, that is, from the earth. In the Scriptures, the Hebrew word for earth or soil (*adamah*) names Adam and all of Adam's sons and daughters down to ourselves. This is how *Genesis* illustrates this etymology:

And the Lord God formed man of the slime of the earth:

> and breathed into his face the breath of life, and man became a living soul. (*Genesis*, 2:7)

Here you have the very transition and the very transcendence from soil to soul. Here also two different aspects of Man come together: on the one hand, "the slime of the earth" refers to the *humus* of the human; but the face of man upon which God breathed life already refers to the personal aspect of Man, that is, human existence as sustained by our relationships with others—other humans, other animals, and the wholly Other, God.

But it is not only in *Genesis* that Man is understood as human, that is, as an earthling; in Greek philosophy too Man is made from the earth:

> Once upon a time, there existed gods but no mortal creatures. When the appointed time came for these also to be born, the gods formed them within the earth out of a mixture of earth and fire and the substances which are compounded from earth and fire. And when they were ready

to bring them to the light, they charged Prometheus and Epimetheus with the task of equipping them and allotting suitable powers to each kind (Plato, *Protagoras*, 320d).

We will return to finish this passage later on. For now, we keep in mind only the fact that the ancient Greeks, like the ancient Israelites, saw man as made from the earth. In Egyptian mythology, we are made of tears; in Babylonian, of blood. They are all right, as you understand.

At this point I noticed that a man who was seated in the front row of the audience (otherwise I would have hardly noticed him, for there was nothing noticeable about him) had turned to his side and was whispering something in the ear of the man seated next to him. It was Jefferey Burnop, a young academic who had produced already a modest number of insipid publications. I was surprised to see him seated next to President Joseph, for when I first met the President—while he was still the present-President and had not yet come to be designated, as he was after the University's calamitous closure, by that moniker that he is widely known today, as the "Immediate Past President"—he had given me what to him must have been a memorized list of arguments, five reasons that make Fenwick so different than all other universities in its league; and one of those "Five Ways" was the fact that Fenwick—"by vocation and by choice," *as he put it*—*actively discouraged its faculty from publishing.* "You can either be a waterpipe or a cistern," *was, if I remember correctly, the analogy he had used.* "Either thoughts go through you, but leave you as they found you, unchanged—but then, my good fellow," *said he, leaning a little forward,* "what good is it to think *at all*?—or the waters of Sophia are collected in the cistern of your soul, and they change you." *The leaning posture which he had adopted recalled that of*

an archangel stooping down from heavens. Talking to him, one had the feeling that he came gliding down form on high in order to make his presidential pronouncements which were thus invested with a supernatural authority. I didn't tell him then, but his image of waters, flowing or standing, had generated in my mind an entirely different thought. The river Jordan supplies with water two lakes that in the language of the Bible are known as the Sea of Galilee, which lets the water pass through her, and the Dead Sea, which selfishly keeps all the water for herself. That, however, was before I had the misfortune of becoming acquainted with the drivel produced by Burnop's pen, or rather by the keyboard of that device he carries with him everywhere. And that, I must add, was not my fault. It wasn't that I went looking for his stuff. I had recently become editor-in-chief of a new academic journal and, in that unfortunate capacity, I was bombarded with the pebbles of his mind. In his case, I would have preferred if he kept them all for himself at the very bottom of his Dead Sea, but they had no weight, and they could not sink, and so they floated on the surface of language.

The astute observer would have noticed that President Joseph had only recently taken a shower—the hair over his neck was still a little wet—even though, by the time of this talk, it was already late afternoon. This observation suggested that he had showered only now that he needed to be among people. Otherwise, he would have spent the day in his customary way, unwashed, unkept, undressed, in the stupor produced by his habitual intoxication.

As Burnop kept talking to President Joseph, I was able to hear only an emphatic "in fact" that Burnop uttered while he absentmindedly straightened with his hand the crease on his trousers over his crossed legs.[9] I admit that he didn't make

---

9   [L.L.] A detail not as insignificant as it might seem at first if one were to consider Freud's comments ("Recommendations in the Technique of Psycho-Analysis" in *Collected Papers*, vol. II) ap-

a good impression on me, not only because he was talking while I was talking, but also because he seemed neither to notice nor therefore to be bothered by the fact that other men, his seniors in office and in age, were forced to sit behind him while he, a much younger-looking fellow with a feeble attempt at growing a beard, was occupying one of the seats of honor. For the sake of my audience, I continued pretending not to notice him.

~*~*~

To whomever might object at this point that, "in fact" we are not made of earth, I respond that we very well know what we are made of and where we come from: *inter faeces et urinam nascimur,* says a Latin phrase that has been attributed at various times to St. Augustine, St. Bernard of Clairvaux, and Seneca, although it does not matter who said it insofar as we all know it to be true—as I had the chance of confirming for myself earlier today on my way to your beautiful campus.[10]

We are born between feces and urine. That's the glorious entrance to the stage of life whether your character is that of a king or of a soldier, of a master or of a slave, of a saint or of a sinner. The world makes such distinctions, but life does not. Hotels, for example, have two entrances, one that receives guests in pomp and grace, and the grim one in the back that admits only the staff. That way there

---

ropos that young philosopher "with leanings towards aesthetic exquisiteness." Dr. William J. Hendel is another example that comes to mind.

10 There is nothing wrong with such subterranean pipes as long as they remain so, that is, hidden. If Freud is to be believed, it is precisely the keeping of those pipes repressed that keeps the City and Civilization going. The achievement of our generation, the one single thing for which we wll be remembered in the future, is taking a powerful fan, a 5G-strong fan and placing it in the sewer. The result is what we call the Internet.

is no contamination. Life, on the other hand, forces us all through the same narrow and dirty tunnel. There is but one gate through which we all have entered into life and it is located between feces and urine.[11]

You will do well to remember this simple truth at all times.

~*~*~

I said this while looking vaguely in the direction of the impertinent Mr. Burnop who was beginning to suspect that my last remarks were directed at him. He quickly reassumed his attention to the lecture and the lecturer behind the lectern, allowing me to continue in a more pacified spirit.

~*~*~

When you envy someone whom you consider to be luckier or happier than you, remember that he too came into life from the same entrance common to us all. When you are afraid of someone, remember the frail baby that he once was (and still is, as we realize at those rare moments of honesty with ourselves). But above all, remember it when you yourself feel too important, when you feel insulted or offended, remember that you were born between feces and urine.

None of the kings had any other beginning of birth.

For all men have one entrance into life, and the like going out (*Wisdom*, 7:5-6).

---

11 With respect to those who think that they are not like the rest of us, common mortals, and instead enter life like Caesars, by means of a caesarean section: I read somewhere recently and with great satisfaction that, avoiding the crucial contact with the bacteria contained in *faeces et urinam* raises significantly their chances for developing later in life autoimmune disorders.

As, therefore, there is but one entrance to life, similarly, there is but one gate through which we all exit and it is as inglorious, I'm afraid, as life's entrance. This time we don't simply go *through* what is smelly and filthy, we *become* that stenchy decomposing corpse, we become organic matter—good fertilizer for the soil. *The soil we came from.* Perhaps it makes a little more sense now? The soil we-are-made-into after our death proves to be the soil we-were-made-from before our birth; the earth to which we return is the proof of the earth from which we originate, as we confess when we call ourselves *humans.* Not long ago, I was a boy playing with dirt, and I am afraid not too long after these lectures I must turn *into* that dirt.

It is our dead skin that becomes dust and accumulates on the surface of furniture; for we die even as we live and, in fact, live because of that gradual process of dying.

2. The Denial of Death

And now I ask: why is our humanity—that is, our earthliness, our mortality—hidden from us? It is true that our society has a marked preference for idealized youth, it asks of us to be as childish as children but without the child-like sincerity; puerile but without purity; everyone wants to remain, like Peter Pan, forever young, foregoing his shadow and remaining trapped in an immaterial—digital, you say—fairy world.

The shadow of death and dying has been banished from our view, both in language and reality. In language—through such expressions as when we hear it said that the police "neutralized" a suspect, that pets are "put down," that animals in labs are "sacrificed," and so on. Montaigne reminds us that such euphemisms have existed at all times and in cultures. In reality—the very place where one would expect to meet death, that is, the funeral, has become paradoxically the least of places one can find him: for there is invariably the grotesque attempt of the morticians to make the dead look life-like. The result is uncanny, but the intention remains clear: to hide death from our eyes. Our society suffers from that contradiction of taking so much care of life and caring so little about death.

I remember that, when I was growing up in Greece, you could always tell who had died in our town, not only because the tolling bells of the Church would announce that a death had occurred in the midst of our community, but also because the body of the dead man would return home to spend its last night on earth with relatives, and the lid of the coffin was always placed in an upright position by the door of the house, so knew which house it was that death had visited this time. The coffin's lid by the door was, as it were, death's calling card, or perhaps his trophy, marking his latest victim and victory, as a proud hunter might display his latest kill. As children we knew that it is only a matter of time before a similar lid would be placed by our door.

To whom is it beneficial that we forget that we are mortals and that death is always with us? Indeed, we begin dying at the moment we are born—even before that, in fact, for many have died before they had a chance to be born. And this astonishing fact, this incontrovertible fact, that we are dying as we speak—*this* we live daily pretending that we do not know.

> Death is the goal of our career, it is, of necessity, what we are aiming for; if it frightens us, how can we take one step forward without trepidation? For common folk the remedy

is not to think about it. But what brutish stupidity can bring on such crass blindness?[12]

What kind of mass and massive superstition makes us believe that if we only pretend that we are not dying, if we only keep going on with our business, as if death couldn't come and interrupt everything and render all our affairs at once what they have always been—worthless, meaningless things, ridiculous dreams and vain efforts—then, somehow death will leave us alone? But that's precisely the point, isn't it? That we don't want our dreams to be rendered ridiculous and our efforts to be proven vain. But they are and so they will be, as indeed they have proved to be for million and millions of other people already dead and for those who are now dying.

A brief but deep silence enveloped the great hall at this moment, such that could only be felt—I almost want to say "heard"—among crowds. It was as if everyone in the room had reached privately and simultaneously the same decision: to keep a moment's silence in memory of the dead or to hold their breadths, trying to determine whether any spirits hovered above us.

~*~*~

There are people—thousands of them, I reckon—for whom today, this day, is their last. When you read in the news of someone's death, look at his picture and think that his death—of which you are currently reading—was as far from his mind then, when that picture was taken, as yours is from you now. Today one of us might have seen a

---

12   Michel de Montaigne, "Through Philosophy We Learn How to Die" in *Selected Essays*, translated by James B. Atkinson and David Sices (Indianapolis: Hackett, 2012), p. 14.

face for the last time—without knowing it. We might have closed the door of our house, walked the dog, or talked to someone for the last time—without having had any idea that this was the last time. Remember also that in the dorms you now sleep in here at Fenwick once slept thousands of others like you before you, who now continue their sleep underground. And remember that the words *dormitory* and *cemetery* are synonyms.

Every night we rehearse our deaths. Consider how the bed is the place of reflection. The bed is the place where my day begins but also the place that, before the day's beginning, before I don the role I have come to play in my interactions with society, I take a reflective stance away from myself and my life. And the bed is the place where I come, at the end of the day, in order to exit the stage. It is from the bed that the temporal categories of *before* and *after* derive their meaning. If I count time by days, then I count by nights; that is, I count by my bedtime. The bed invokes not only the beginning and the end of each day, but also the beginning and end of *all* our days. Most of us are born in a bed and, if lucky, we will die in a bed, something that is rehearsed every night when we go to bed, in that simulation of death we call sleeping. This is why self-reflection—which, although characteristic of our humanity, is *not* a natural attitude for the human being who only intends something else other than himself (I use the language of phenomenology here)—feels natural at bedtime. It is while I am in bed, preparing to fall asleep or having just woken up, that I become "naturally" reflective, as in bed I can assume that crucial distance which shall enable me to move from actor to spectator and see myself in the drama that unfolds on the stage of the Theater of the Everyday.

It is from this point of view—from the ground—that we need to look back and evaluate everything and every action in life, judging how it measures up in relation to the ground—and the grave.

Golden lads and girls all must,

As chimney-sweepers, come to dust (Shakespeare, *Cymbeline*, Act IV, scene 2).

Here you have two antithetical views of death: one, secular, seeks to hide our mortality from our eyes, the very eyes it bedazzles with virtual visions of eternal youth; the other, remarkably ecclesial, takes the form of a perpetual reminder of death, a *memento mori* but without despair, for it expects the resurrection of the dead.

> [T]here can be no denying that "our cities are erected atop burial grounds." So too, one might argue, are our churches—a fact which ought not to be glibly dismissed. But while the former devise means of diverting us from the burial of the dead, the latter build belltowers to proclaim it. This is a stark contrast. Civilization distracts and, to the degree to which it can, protects us from mortality. The church—with its incessant *now and at the hour of our deaths* and *to dust you shall returns*—thrusts it before us. Which ought the philosopher to prefer?[13]

3. Philosophical Immortality

If you have read only as far as the first paragraph of that essay by Montaigne to which I have already been referring, you will see that the good Seigneur attributes to Cicero a certain definition of philosophy as the preparation to death.[14] (This is, then, how one is to imagine

---

13   Matthew Clemente, *Bacchus Agonistes* (Senex Press, 2025), p. 5. A text yet unwritten at the time of this lecture, which I nevertheless anticipated—or, perhaps, prophesied—would come.

14   Cicero, *Tusculan Disputations*, 1. 30: *Tota enim philosophorum vita . . . commentatio mortis est.*

Lady Philosophy, as crying to us every time we encounter her the warning "Prepare to die, mortal!") Cicero himself borrowed it from Socrates who, as he was preparing to die, explained to his friends, that at this, his last hour, he had nothing to fear, for as a philosopher he had spent all his life doing precisely this, preparing to die. For, as he argues in Plato's *Phaedo*, if "the philosopher's occupation consists precisely in the freeing and separating of soul from body," "Then, it is a fact that true philosophers make dying their profession" (67d-e). Montaigne tells us why that is: "inasmuch as study and contemplation draw our souls out of us to some extent, and busying it outside of the body, this is a kind of apprenticeship and likeness of death."[15]

There are two modes by which we humans exist: either in action or in reflection; either we are the actors of the action or else we are its spectators, but rarely both at the same time and with respect to the same thing, You can look back and reflect upon your actions in the past, in which case you become the spectator of your actions, but spectator and actor are not synchronized, since one is in the present and the other in the past, and it is nearly impossible for them to be contemporaries.[16] The condition of reflection is then the suspension of the world of action. In order to reflect upon the world, one must extricate oneself from it, as if stepping back in order to look

---

15   Michel de Montaigne, "Through Philosophy We Learn How to Die," p. 11.

16   "Impossible"—but what is impossible for mortals is not so for Proust (or for literature). Although it might be assigned to all literature as a universal characteristic (achieved by individual writers to various degrees), it is in Proust's prose, in particular, that it becomes possible to experience the intertwining of description (action) and reflection and the fusion of the tale with its telling. For more see the fourth of my *Fenwick Essays on the Art of Literature* (Boston: Senex Press, 2026).

at it (that is, to make it one's *object*) and, similarly, in order to reflect upon oneself (by objectifying oneself)—which is what philosophy principally does—one must separate himself from himself, a separation that simulates the separation of soul from body, that is, death.

Insofar as philosophers have made dying their occupation, philosophers are professional mortals.[17] *How morbid!* you may think. Shouldn't philosophy rather focus on life and living? What good is it to be wise, to have wisdom (if philosophy is the pursuit of *sophia*), what good is this wisdom if you can only find it—like Orpheus finds his wife Eurydice—among the dead or if you can find it only by dying?

> Either it is totally impossible to acquire knowledge, or it is only possible after death... (*Phaedo*, 66e).

That's the famous Socratic either/or. Montaigne has a different take:

> In truth, either philosophy is a waste of time or its purpose really is our happiness and it should, in everything it does, bring us closer to living well.

Very well, then. On the subject of living well, the first lesson is to learn to die.

~*~*~

"Another Silenus!" I overheard Burnop saying to President Jospeh. His unsolicited comment referred to Herodotus' story about King Midas who is said to have captured a drunk satyr in order to extract the secret of life from him. With the satyr's initial resistance bent ("Oh, you wretched ephemeral race!

---

17   The Christian monk, as the philosopher par excellence, is similarly a professional mortal: "A monk is a mourning soul that both asleep and awake is unceasingly occupied with the remembrance of death." St. John Climacus, *The Ladder of Divine Ascent*, 1:4; Holy Transfiguration Monastery, Boston, 2001, p. 4.

Why do you ask what would be more expedient for you not to know?"), *Silenus replied that it would be best for man not to be born, but if he already has, the second-best thing is to die as soon as possible. I would like to take this opportunity to remind the reader that that same Socrates whom I had just mentioned in my lecture was often compared to a satyr in Plato's dialogues.*

~*~*~

The first thing I must tell you is that you will die. If you begin living and, even worse, if you begin thinking from any other point of departure, you waste your time. If you want to live, you must begin with the realization that you are dying. In Montaigne's words, *you are either dead or dying*—"you are dead after life; but while you are alive you are dying."

Only now can you begin living because, strangely, paradoxically, death has provided you with a point, a term, a terminal, in which everything terminates, and such a term functions as a point of orientation that organizes space and time for you and makes action possible. As much as you can't begin to run if you don't know *to-ward* what you are running—that is, in which direction—as much as you can't run, then, without a finish line, it is the term and the terminal that defines the course. And when you desire a career and when you submit your *curriculum vitae* you understand life, even if you don't realize it, as a running course (*currere*, to run).

The first characteristic of this orientation toward death (the old *memento mori*) is that it provides a definition to your perspective (the definition that makes perspective possible and thus that all-important vision that lies at the foundation of knowledge), it gives shape to things, it gives the right proportions to things and makes your actions meaningful.

> It is not certain where Death awaits us, so let us await it everywhere. To think of death beforehand is to think of our liberty. Whoever learns how to die has learned how not to be a slave. Knowing how to die frees us from all subjection and constraint.[18]

4. Posthumous Living

What Montaigne argues here is the idea of *posthumous living*; the suggestion that often an encounter with death leads to an initiation into life. This is, for example, one of the points, if not the main point, made by Thomas Mann in *The Magic Mountain*. A story that takes place in a sanatorium, a place that is a cross between a hotel and a hospital. It resembles, if only by inversion, like a reflection, Book XI of Homer's *Odyssey* where Odysseus, in order to return home to his life and his wife, must first, like Orpheus on a similar quest, descend to Hades. He must, that is, undergo a symbolic death, so that the much-desired and sought-after return to Ithaca can be achieved posthumously. *The Magic Mountain* is such a *nekyia*—in both senses of a *katabasis* and a necromancy.

Perhaps a better example to illustrate posthumous living is that of Ebenezer Scrooge, the miserable miser in Charles Dicken's *A Christmas Carol*. Scrooge was living before the three ghosts visited him that night before Christmas, but he became alive and was able to enjoy himself only after the ghost of Christmas Yet to Come had shown him the tombstone with his own name engraved on

---

18 Michel de Montaigne, "Through Philosophy We Learn How to Die," p. 17.

it. His joy on Christmas morning is the joy of a man who has survived his own death.

You see it wouldn't be fair to discuss health or wealth, pleasures or pains, without taking these two facts into consideration. It wouldn't be good to consider how good it is to have a lot of goods unless you knew, and you remembered, that they are no good to you beyond the grave, and that their value is relative to the use they can be put to in this life. And the same relative character must be assigned not only to wealth but also to health, and to knowledge, and to science, and to everything else. You should evaluate everything by asking how it stands in relation to death. Will it withstand death or is it useful in teaching you how to die? For to live well must ultimately mean knowing how to die—knowing, first of all, how to deal with the certainty, with the facticity of your death. For one who doesn't know how to die well lives badly. "No man can live well once but he that could live twice."[19]

5. Mechanical Immortality

With the advent of technology, however, and especially bio-technology, some people, emboldened by these advances, have begun flirting, and I am afraid in earnest, with the idea of a man-made deathlessness. Man wants again to become immortal. I say "again" because this is the second time that Man has succumb to the temptation to become "like gods." The first, as we shall see tomorrow, took place in a Garden.

But is a deathless life livable? If by "deathless" you mean "longer" then of course and with pleasure! But

---

19   Sir Thomas Browne, *Religio Medici*, Part 1, sec. 42.

deathless means something more: it means endless.[20] And endless is a very long time. For example, would you get married in such a deathless life, realizing, after the first few centuries of marriage to your lovely and equally immortal spouse, that you are to live together, not "till death do us part," but *forever*? If people today can make that promise, and if they can honor the commitment that follows from that promise, that's because death does part them from each other at some point. And, following this example, would not any other action that requires commitment on our part, a commitment of our time, become similarly impossible in a deathless existence? Why undertaking learning a language today if you will be around forever? There is no urgency, no need attached to this today anymore. You can do it tomorrow or a hundred years from now, what difference does it make?

It makes no difference, for there is no difference anymore between life and death. That is to say, as soon as there is no difference between life and death, then nothing makes a difference.[21] I don't suggest, however, that death is one pole of a dialectical opposition between life and death and that, if not for death, life would have been meaningless. That is, I don't use these terms—life and death—absolutely, but as conditioned by human existence

---

20 Endless means also without the possibility of stopping man from committing atrocious evil to himself or to others. Thus, some of the Church Fathers saw in the introduction of death in the narrative of *Genesis*, not only a punishment but also a merciful expedient that puts an end to evil and suffering.

21 And this in two very different senses; for it is also true of a Christian for whom, because "whether we live or die we belong to Christ" (*Romans* 14:8), there is really no difference between life and death and, therefore, nothing makes no difference as well. However, Christian indifference leads to fortitude, when suffering pain, and to temperance, when suffering pleasure; worldly indifference, on the other hand, leads only to insufferable boredom.

in the world. What I am trying to say is that for us, such as
we are, *mortals*, destined to die, there is no other point of
departure to make sense of what it means to be a human
being than by taking into account these certainties, these
facts that make our facticity—the facts that make *us*:

a)   You will die;
b)   You don't know when.

6. The Plutocracy of the Underworld

We began with the *humus* of our humanity and we
moved to the idea of a life lived posthumously; it is time to
visit now the third link of this conceptual cluster—*exhumation*. The exhumation of those precious metals and
stones that serve as the foundation of wealth. But first,
please remember that the god of the underworld is Plutos
(his name means wealth) and those who worship him are
already in his kingdom.[22] He is the rich one (*Dis Pater*
in the Roman pantheon) not only because it is from the
underworld that the human riches are taken, but because
every mortal who dies makes death's kingdom richer. In

---

22   [L.L.] It is unfortunate that Manoussakis's papophile (cf., "The
     Heresy of Anti-Papism") and monarchical (cf., "Primacy and
     the Holy Trinity") affinities prevent him from citing Milton. For
     Milton made this point better than any philosopher by writing
     the following lines about Mammon:

   Mammon, the least erected Spirit that fell
   From heav'n, for ev'n in heav'n his looks and thoughts
   Were always downward bent, admiring more
   The riches of Heav'ns pavement, trod'n Gold,
   Then aught divine or holy else enjoy'd
   In vision beatific: by him first
   Men also, and by his suggestion taught
   Ransack'd the Center, and with impious hands
   Rifl'd the bowels of thir mother Earth
   For Treasures better hid. (*Paradise Lost*, I. xx)

this mythological association, death and wealth are inextricably connected.

The people who have invested the greatest hope and resources in attaining a mechanical simulation of immortality are, as you may expect, the rich. And it is the rich not because they have a lot to invest in the search for immortality, but because they have much to lose by their mortality. The more you are attached to your possessions, the more you are possessed by them, the more painful it will be when the time comes to lose them. A man, on the other hand, who has nothing—one of those homeless people in our streets whose death goes unreported—what does he lose? By death he *gains* a grave—which is more than he had in life. Death robs the rich of their wealth, and against that robber they are powerless, since they can't take anything with them beyond the grave, while in the grave everything they had amassed becomes useless.

> Do not place hope upon wrongdoing,
> And do not set your desire on stealing;
> *If wealth flows* [increases],
> Do not put your heart on it (Psalm 62:10/61:11).

Do not put your heart—that is, do not trust or believe, do not give any credit—to wealth.[23] Why not? Because it is *flowing*. Why does the Psalm speak of wealth as *flowing*? Because property does not have a proper owner. Yesterday was someone else's, today yours, and tomorrow

---

23   In English we speak about one's *creed*, that is, a set of beliefs. The word comes from the Latin *credo*, to believe. But *credo* itself is a shorten form of "cor-do" (*cor* is Latin for heart, as in *coeur* and *corazón*, and *do* is from the verb *dare* which means "to give"). You understand now that when people throughout the ages repeated the first words of the Creed, "Credo in unum Deo," they were not so much making an abstract profession of a theological formula as they were saying "I put my heart" or, as we would say today, "I put my trust" in the One God, the almighty Father.

another's. Yesterday, today, tomorrow—these are temporal categories of time conceived precisely in its flowing,
as Heraclitus imagined it, as a river flowing from past to
present and from here emptying in the delta of the future.
That's the river in whose waters no one can step twice,
for it constantly changes, it is never the same.[24] We are
in the river of time, and we are flowing with it. Whatever
we might acquire on the way flows with us—which means
that we can never possess anything in any real sense as
long as time still flows, and once time has stopped, then
one is dead and has no use of any property. This is the
current of currency.

> The course of mortal life is like this. Human beings are
> born, they live, they die; as some die, others are born, and
> as they die in their turn others again rise up. There is suc-
> cession, arrival, departure; none of them abide. Can we hold
> onto anything? Is there anything that does not run through
> our fingers? Or anything that does not disappear into the
> ocean, like the rain that gathered to form the stream? The
> river surfaced suddenly as rainwater accumulated, swelled
> by many drips from many showers, but it vanishes into the
> sea and we cannot distinguish it, any more than we could
> see it before it was formed by the rain. So too the human
> race is formed from hidden sources and flows out into the
> open but then disappears into death.[25]

You cannot own anything, and everything you have
acquired (with God knows how much pain and effort),
including your own flesh, you will have to return upon
exiting. This world is not our home, we are here tempo-
rarily, on our way (*homo viator*) to our last and lasting

24　Fragment 91: ποταμῷ γὰρ οὐκ ἔστιν ἐμβῆναι δὶς τῷ αὐτῷ.
25　St. Augustine, *Expositions of the Psalms*, translated by Maria
　　Boulding, New York: New City Press, Psalm 109 (volume
　　III/19), p. 284.

stop: we cannot pretend to be the owners when we pay, with our lives, rent.

7. Holy Fools

There is a category of saint called the "holy fool" who becomes holy by his folly. Folly, of course, is the highest form of wisdom. For, as such saints know well, our ultimate trap is pride (because our ultimate threat is the self) and so some choose to put on a play by which they fool everybody into believing that they are fools and, in so doing, become jesters for the sake of the Kingdom. These fools become fools *willingly* as others *willingly* choose poverty—Christianity has this trick by which she turns the voluntary poor and the voluntary fool into heirs of an unexpected wealth and wisdom. St. Basil the Fool, for instance, began as an assistant in a cobbler's shop in Russia. One day, a customer came to order a pair of boots, good, sturdy boots, such that it might last for a long time. But how foolish he proved to be when Basil the Fool foretold that he, the customer, was destined to die the next day. Again, they say that Lazarus, after spending four days in the tomb, never laughed again except once, when he saw a man stealing some pottery. When they asked him why he was laughing—for remember, this is the man who spent four days dead in a tomb—he said: "I saw some earth stealing some more earth." How different our lives would be if we were to adopt a similar attitude and were to ask ourselves, "What would Lazarus see if he was looking at me"?

Allow me to illustrate my point with a parable from the Gospels. It is the story known as the Parable of the Rich Fool (Luke 12:16-21):

> There was a wealthy man whose land yielded an abundant harvest. He thought to himself: "What shall I do, for I do not have sufficient space to store my crops?" Then he said, "This is what I will do. I will pull down my barns and build larger ones, where I will store my grain and other produce, and shall say to myself, 'Now you have an abundance of goods stored up for many years to come. Relax, eat, drink, and be merry!'"

(Please note that every time the rich fool speaks, he speaks to himself; he has no-one to speak to, no-one to share anything with—not even words— that's why his gains overflow his storerooms. Greed and selfishness go naturally together.)

> But God said to Him, "You fool! This very night your life will be required of you and who then will get to enjoy the fruit of your labors?" That is how it will be for the one who stores up treasures for himself yet fails to become rich in the sight of God.

"You fool! This very night your life will be required of you." How can it be "required" (that is, taken away from him), *unless it wasn't his to begin with?* You are not your life. You are alive. You have life and you have it, as Anaximander suggests, *on loan.* A loan to be paid back in full upon death. A *mort*gage.

8. Beings and Being

Anaximander's fragment[26] is one of the earliest utterances of philosophy and unexpectedly dark for a Greek. It says that everything that exists—and, insofar as it exists, is *a* being and not *the* Being, anything that *has* being or

---

26 Fragment 1: ἐξ ὧν δὲ ἡ γένεσίς ἐστι τοῖς οὖσι, καὶ τὴν φθορὰν εἰς ταῦτα γίνεσθαι κατὰ τὸ χρεών διδόναι γὰρ αὐτὰ δίκην καὶ τίσιν ἀλλήλοις τῆς ἀδικίας κατὰ τὴν τοῦ χρόνου τάξιν.

existence, but cannot claim to *be* itself life or existence—has committed a terrible crime for which it must atone or, rather, must be punished by returning to the same nothingness from which it emerged when it came to be. And it is the very possibility of punishment—of *our* punishment, for I speak of us mortals as well—it is the very possibility of our punishment that is the proof of our guilt and crime. That life *can* and *will* be taken away from us is the very proof that it wasn't ours to begin with. And if we do have it, that can only mean one thing: *that we stole it.* By the very act of living, we are caught red-handed committing the crime of existing.

We meet here one of the earliest "collective memories" of humanity: the memory of a primordial crime and of an ancient or ancestral guilt, the memory of a sin that is original, that is, contemporaneous to the origins of our race and perhaps, as Anaximander articulated in his own language, of having an origin, of having originated. That man has always had pretensions to existence and sought to usurp it for himself has been testified to by the literature of every ancient culture. In *Genesis* it is the promise of "becoming like Gods" (3:5) that prompts the crime that brings about the punishment of mortality. In other words, we die because we tried to be like God. In the story of Prometheus, the idea is similar: Prometheus—the hero who acts on behalf of the human race and as its benefactor—*steals* the fire that had, up until then, belonged only to the gods and gives it to human beings allowing them to survive, that is, to live. It is easy to see here how fire is an image of civilization, but also of life as sustained by civilization, not nature, that is, man's life as sustained by man himself. Fire is artificial light and artificial heat, as opposed to the light and the heat provided *naturally* by the sun. Artificial and artisan. Prometheus' punishment is to be tied to a rock—prefiguring the Sisyphean life of a man who is tied to this rock that is our planet—and have his liver—a vital organ, representing one's vitality—eaten daily by an eagle.

There much to be said of Anaximander's dark saying—especially, what makes the difference between life as, in his view, a crime and life, as we tend to see it, as a gift—but there is only one more feature of this saying that interests us in our present inquiry. This cycle of becoming, coming to being from nothingness, non-being to being and returning back to non-being, lurks somewhere behind another idea that some of you might be familiar with, namely, the idea of reincarnation or *metempsychosis*, which is debated, for the first time, on the last day of Socrates' life in Plato's *Phaedo* (70c-72e). The idea of reincarnation is, in essence, a theory of maintaining equilibrium between living and death by a continuous process of recycling that provides for the continuation of all things and of the human race. Your grandfather dies but your grandson is born.[27] What exactly is recycled is not immediately clear. Traditionally it is thought that the souls are recycled, but this must be even more the case for matter, thus making this theory the forerunner in some oblique way, to the principle of mass conservation (Lavoisier). There is an economy of both matter and spirit

---

27   I like to think of all the hospitals in Boston as airports for the souls that land and depart from there daily. They must be very busy spots in the souls' transmigrations. There are other similarities between births and deaths. When a pregnant woman goes to labors a midwife might be called to assist. Socrates called his own philosophical method *maieutic* meaning midwifery, an art he claims to have learned from his mother who practiced it. But there are also midwives of death. In Sardinia and other parts of Sicily there was believed to have existed a woman or rather the office of a woman, called *L'Accabadora*, a midwife of death who would be called by the relatives of a dying person to help them, with her little olive-wood mallet, pass on to the next world.

whose regulation has always been assumed by the City (the Polis) that gives a political dimension to death.

For the ancients the best illustration of the connection between death and wealth was the myth of Sisyphus. For Sisyphus, when he was alive, was "the most successful among men" according to Homer (Iliad VI, 153):

> Sisyphus who, according to Homer, is κέρδιστος ἀνδρῶν, that is the "most gaining among men," a reference to capital gains he was able to make as the founder of Corinth and the first to control the Isthmus of Corinth thus becoming (as Ruskin observes in his *Queen of Air*) "the type of transit, transfer, or trade." It is in the underworld that Sisyphus finds out the true meaning of the proverbial phrase about the "rolling stone" which not only, as we all know, "gathers no moss" but also never finds rest in all eternity.[28]

For in Hades, as you know, Sisyphus is the most human of men, the man closest to the earth, as Milton's Mammon is "the least erected Spirit," for in being eternally condemned to roll uphill a boulder only to see his efforts lost in vain as the boulder rolls back down, he is also the man who has eaten the most dust.

9. The Value of Wealth

Before I speak on the value of the wealth, a word on the meaning of the word "value." It comes from *valor* and *valere,* to be well, strong, and healthy. The Latin equivalent of the Greek ὑγιαίνω. "To be 'valuable', therefore," as Ruskin writes, "is 'to avail towards life.' A truly valuable or availing thing is that which leads to life with its whole strength."[29] A valuable thing is "strong for life" as a val-

---

28 Jean-Luc Beauchard, *The Fruit of Death*, (Boston: Senex Press, 2024), p.17. (Cf. fn13 above.)
29 John Ruskin, *Ad Valorem*, p. 93.

iant person is "strong in life." Wealth, then should serve health—that is, making us whole, but whole to capacity; for beyond that limit, you no longer make yourself strong but weak. As overfeeding a body beyond its need and capacity for food makes it not healthier but unhealthy and ill, so all wealth that is beyond our capacity to use does not make us wealthier but sick.

For political economists, however, "to be wealthy is to have a large stock of useful articles, or the means of purchasing them"[30]—a definition worth examining, for it provides us with an occasion to think the following three questions:

a) What does it mean *to have*?
b) How much is needed for one's possessions to qualify as *large*?
c) What is *useful*?

You have that which you use and for as long as you use it, for although there might be a very large stock of useful and valuable articles hidden in the secret chambers of a pyramid, it cannot be said that the dead Pharaoh *has* them, for he doesn't have any use for them, nor can we say that he owns them, for both he and them are owned by the tomb. Or to use another example closer to home, so to speak, with which you are all, I am sure, familiar: in the beautiful chapel of St. Elsewhere which adorns the center of your campus, there is a silver reliquary within which lie the relics of the venerable founder of your university, John Fenwick, S.J. Does he possess the silver reliquary, or does it contain him?

Possession is determined by the ability to use, so *that* which one cannot use, one does not have; and if he has it beyond its use, he abuses it. If he is not using it, he is

---

30 John Stuart Mill, *Principles of Political Economy*, "Preliminary Remarks."

abusing it, for by having it and keeping it, he prevents it from being used. To prevent the use of the useful is to abuse it. But to prevent the use of the useful from those who need it is to abuse *them*. "What a person has, another cannot have."[31] Or, put more bluntly, "no one puts bread into his belly without depriving the belly of another."[32] Therefore, any "large stock of useful articles" is ultimately possession of stolen goods. If we always remember this simple truth, that money is only the means to an end, we will not ask people, as we do now, how much they are making. What we rather ought to ask of others and ourselves is to what purpose do we spend.

With age, money takes on an additional value as that which affords a certain degree of independence. It is not so much a question of simply having money, but of having one's own money. But what about one's dependance on money, the very money, ironically, with which one sought to buy one's independence? One has simply exchanged masters. Before he was dependent on those who provided him with money, now he is dependent on money itself and, ultimately, on those who "make" money for him—his employer or customer. The only independence with respect to money is freedom from money, not the illusion of freedom bought with money. Free, that is, truly independent is he who does not need money and who can provide for his needs himself with the labor of his hands and mind. Free is he who needs less, not he who has *more*. For the more one has of this "more-having sauce that makes us hunger more" (*Macbeth*, act IV, scene 3), the more he hungers for more.

---

31 John Stuart Mill, *Principles of Political Economy*, "Preliminary Remarks."
32 Matthew Clemente, *Bacchus Agonistes*, (Boston: Senex Press, 2024), p. 3. (Cf. fn13 & fn28 above.)

I would like to leave you at the end of this, the first of my Fenwick Lectures, with four pieces of advice with respect to our relation to wealth and money summarized in the following:

10. Four Principles of Economy

a)   Before you make it in the world—before you prepare to conquer the world—learn first to be happy in it. Because if you do that, and you are able to be happy in it, you may discover that you don't have to conquer it, you don't have to possess it, and that will save you a lot of trouble (and maybe a little bit of money as well).

b)   Seek not greater wealth but simpler pleasures—that is, a constant and faithful pleasure.

c)   Don't squander your life on making more money before you learn how to make much of it; and,

d)   Put first among your possessions, self-possession.

By self-possession I mean freedom from one's voluntary servitude to wealth; hence there are two senses by which one can understand "financial independence." It feels good, no doubt, to be able to buy what one wants; but why assume that this is as far as you can go, when you can go a step farther and discover that it feels *better*, in fact, to be able to *not* buy what you do *not* need. When you begin to cultivate little by little and in small things such an attitude of voluntary poverty, you delight in your self-mastery and in being now financially independent from the constraints of finances themselves. In short, learn how to have enough and don't desire always more, for if you desire always more, you will never have enough, no matter how much, and you will never be happy. To close with a verse from another Psalm: "Better is the little to the just, than the great riches of the wicked" (Ps. 36/37:16).[33]

---

33 Psalm 36 (in the LXX) is in its entirety a little treatise on eco-
    nomics, and it can be said to summarize nicely what the Bible
    has to say on economy in general.

The Second Day

The Rise of Anthropos

*O*n the morning of the second day, Louis Light, the President's mercurial messenger, came to my rooms. Apparently, there was the general complaint that the first day's lecture had been inordinately long. And yet the proposed theme of the second lecture necessitated a still longer treatment, if I was to be given the time to treat the second term as completely as the first, for I was intending to trace it to no less than three main etymological derivations. (As any of my students would tell you, my dear Reader, I am notorious for my penchant for etymologies.) My fears reached the President who, wise as Solomon, decided that, in order that I might be accorded the freedom to develop my subject at the length necessary to satisfy my scholarly standards, yet without subjecting his community to a trial beyond human bearing, the second lecture must be divided into three parts, each part to be delivered at three different times during the day: The first at the Terce Hour, the second at the Sext, and the third at the None.

The three parts of the Second Lecture, therefore, are designated by the corresponding hour during which they were delivered.

At the Terce

(That is, around 9:00 a.m.)

*A*round *nine o'clock in the morning I stood up, looked at the hall full of my audience, and said:* The human being is a *position* and a *look.*[34]

The Greek word for the human being is *anthropos* (a word that you may recognize in such derivatives as anthropology, anthropomorphism, lycanthropy, and anthropophagy). Whereas the Latin word—human, *humus*—names man after his origins, the Greek *anthropos* speaks of man's destiny. I can venture to offer you no less than three distinct etymologies of ἄνθρωπος:

a) *Anthropos* is that being who rises up, or raises himself up, from the earth by standing up and looking up [ἄνω θρώσκω > ὁράω]. That's a much more sophisticated and nuanced way of saying what the "homo erectus" tries to say: the up-standing being,

---

34 [L.L.] I think that now might be the appropriate time to add a note on Fr. Manoussakis's physical appearance. Those who knew him in person before his untimely demise would surely remember that Manoussakis, as an Orthodox priest, had kept the ancestral look of his forefathers in the Greek priesthood, wearing his hair long and messy, with a bushy beard, and a corpulent body that seemed to approximate, as closely as human figure can, a three-aisled Byzantine Basilica with a dome. When he opened his mouth—and his seldom shut it—he spoke with a heavy Russian accent (though he was indeed Greek in virtue and in vice), the result, no doubt, of having been dedicated to and named after St. John the Russian.

the vertical mammal. Why does man stand up if not in order to see? Orthograde posture was only possible by bipedalism—the former was motivated by the curiosity of looking up at the stars, the latter led to the infamous fall into the well of Thales, history's first stargazer and philosopher.

b) *Anthropos* is that being which, because it can stand up and look up, not only sees but also "considers and observes," that is, the being that reflects, the reflecting being. The prefix *an-* in *anthropos* in this case is taken to mean not ἄνω (up) as in the first etymology, but rather ἀνά which functions as the prefix *re-* in *repetition*. (This etymology is given by Socrates in Plato's *Cratylus*, 399.) Yet, if man is the reflecting and remembering being—recollection being at the center of Platonic metaphysics—that is only because man has been scattered and dis-membered by desire. And,

c) *Anthropos* is the being that looks-like-a-human (ἄνδρωπος, from ἄνδρας and ὀπός), that is, the being that looks or faces-at-a-human. We hear here an echo of the "face of man" we read about in *Genesis*, the face upon which God breathes in order to bring man to life and the face-to-face relationship that such a breathing suggests. This third derivation of the etymology of *anthropos*, since it already raises the concept of relationship, will lead us naturally to the third of my Fenwick lectures: Man as *persona/prosopon*, that is, as the relational being.

1. Looking Up and Falling Down

Anthropos means ἄνω θρώσκω: to look up. Here you have a position (up) and a look: a look that is directed upwards. Upwards is relative to the speaker's position; the subject who, by looking up, by understanding and speaking of the direction of his look as upward, that is, *higher* in relation to himself, must, therefore, understand his position as lower, as lying down. I don't think you can look up unless you are down. *Anthropos* then presupposes the human—that is, the being who came from earth (*humus*).

Anthropos means the earthly being has risen up, has emerged from the ground and can now stand up and walk, instead of crawl (although he still crawls until he learns how to walk—for each one of us in our individual lives repeats and rehearses the evolution of the species— as did the Theanthropos who, in being born as Anthropos returned to a cave) and, because he can now stand up and walk, man can now see, he now has the look, the vision, sight, even though he has sacrificed the smell, which is taste, that is, the ability of *sapio*, the ability of *sapere*, that is, of savoring and of being savvy, for the *homo sapiens* can be sapient only so long as he remains close to the ground. Man stands up and by doing so, his eyes—not his mouth or nose—become the predominant channels through which he takes in the world around him; eyes and ears, the senses of distance and difference, not mouth and nose, the senses of proximity and intimacy—the latter suggest an entirely different kind of knowledge that is lost to us. Vision presents us with a world of things—even persons are presented in their thinghood. Hearing, on the other hand, gives us the person and what is personal in the person, namely the voice which, even though we cannot see, we can hear. I suspect that most of us, if we had the choice between going deaf or going blind, would, regrettably, choose to lose the sound of others' voices rather than their appearances, for we are, after all, spellbound by the world of things. This is a fundamental distortion of the world that characterizes the oculocentric predicament of our tele-technologies.

That other kind of knowledge—a whole other capacity of knowing—has been almost entirely lost because our technology, our culture, our civilization are all *oculocentric*. And because they are based on vision, and vision is, as I called it, a sense of distance (that is, it presupposes distance and creates distances by placing objects at various distances from itself and each other within the optical field, so that the categories "far" and "near" are the ones that organize the field of vision), all our technology is, therefore, tele-technological. The Greek adjective *tele-* means in or from a distance, thus television and telephone means to see and speak from far off distances, telegram and telegraph to write from far off distances.

But technology, even before it became tele-technological, was made possible by that rising up of the *anthropos* (although to some degree it always sought to move away from the body and its limitations—technology is motivated by the thrust of *excarnation*, that is, the very opposite of incarnation—it is, in this sense, anti-Christic). By standing up, man liberated his hands from serving as feet and thus was given, for the first time, the *hand*; what the hand does is handle and manipulate so that man has, because of the hand, *techne*: skillful hands that make artifacts. The hands of a man are not used as tools, as body parts are for other animals; the hands of a man are not tools because they are themselves tool-making and tool-handling. And because man has the handling hand, he no longer needs to use his mouth to carry or store things as animals do; thus the mouth can be used to carry and store words and ideas. The speaking mouth, the instruments of speech and language (*logos*), gives man that -*logy* of techno-logy (and many more -*logies*). So, both, *techne* and *logos*, technology in its totality, resulted from man rising from the dust and becoming *Anthropos*.

As you can see, there is so much that man gains by standing up. But what does he stand to lose?

2. Two Kinds of Knowledge: Olfactory and Ocular

I have already mentioned that Man's upright position favors the sense of sight and vision above all other senses. Other animals, even animals known for their keen eyesight, like cats, prefer to rely on the sense of smell. Appearances, you see, deceive. A good disguise and professional make-up might render an actor unrecognizable to his friends and even to his family, but it won't fool his dog. I have read that animals and even plants can detect whether one really intends or only pretends to harm them. Can they read our minds? Or is it perhaps that our state of mind betrays itself through chemical or other signals that *they* are able to detect but we are not because we have learned to rely on words (on our own system of signification) instead of those natural signals which seem to be a natural language. Otherwise, we would know, for example, how a lie smells. I am, therefore, inclined to believe those desert fathers who have claimed—and some still do—that sin stinks and that one can distinguish different sins by their distinct odor. The nose knows with a knowledge superior to that of the eyes, as it is preserved in saints and animals, thus suggesting that ocular knowledge is particular to the fallen man. But also, the nose can grow "blind"[35] to our own odors, especially when one persists in the foulness of sin for the sake of comfort, just

---

35 Blind, deaf, mute—we have words for the loss of that which we value most: to see, to hear, to speak; but we do not even have

as animals in a stable basking in the heat of their feces are not bothered by the stench.

A good sense of smell, on the other hand, can help an animal perceive farther than human eyes can see and I mean farther not only in space but also in time, farther into the past and farther into the future—for it is by smell that a dog can sense the onset of a disease as yet undiagnosed and undetected, and can tell who has been in a room hours or even days before, when you can only see what is in front of your eyes at present. Don't forget Odysseys' dog, the only creature that recognized his Master upon his return to Ithaca. If man in his epistemology is unable to move beyond the present, that is because he can believe only what he sees but he can only see what is *presented* to him, that is, only the *present*. Smell and taste, on the other hand, can give much more efficient and effective access to the past—as in the famous episode of the little madeleines in Proust's *In Search of Lost Time*:

> [O]ne day in winter, on my return home, my mother, seeing that I was cold, offered me some tea, a thing I did not ordinarily take. I declined at first, and then, for no particular reason, changed my mind. . . . And soon, mechanically dispirited after a dreary day with the prospect of a depressing morrow, I raised to my lips a spoonful of the tea in which I had soaked a morsel of the cake. No sooner had the then liquid mixed with the crumbs touched my palate than a shiver ran through me, and I stopped, intent upon the extraordinary thing that was happening to me.

What follows is nothing less than a quasi-religious conversion, a mystical experience of smell and taste:

> An exquisite pleasure had invaded my senses, something isolated, detached, with no suggestion of its origin. And at

---

a word for a "blind mouth"—to use Milton's expression—or a "deaf nose."

once the vicissitudes of life had become indifferent to me,
its disasters innocuous, its brevity illusory—the new sensation having had the effect, which love has, of filling me with
a precious essence; or rather this essence was not in me, it
was me. I had ceased to feel mediocre, contingent, mortal.
Whence could it have come to me, this all-powerful joy?

The remaining seven volumes of the novel are the answer
to this question. What interests us in the present discussion, however, is that it is a joy that is not intellectual or
cerebral, it is not a vision but a taste, a foretaste, if you
prefer, of an eschatological happiness, for it defies the
death that engulfs history and its endless accumulation
of yesterdays. Here the past is not lost and lost time is
regained:

> [W]hen from a long-distant past nothing subsists, after the
> people are dead, after the things are broken and scattered,
> taste and smell alone, more fragile but more enduring, more
> immaterial, more persistent, more faithful, remain poised a
> long time, like souls, remembering, waiting, hoping, amid
> the ruins of all the rest; and bear unflinchingly, on tiny and
> almost impalpable drops of their essence, the vast structure
> of recollection.

3. The City in Place of the Garden

In yesterday's lecture I presented to you man in his
mortality. Already then, the first feeble efforts at some
kinds of immortality were suggested. One was *mechanical immortality* pursued by the rich, since death to them is
a particularly acute question by virtue of the possessions
they risk losing. The other was *philosophical immortality*
articulated by Plato in his arguments for the immortality
of the soul in the *Phaedo*. A third kind of immortality was

what prompted man to build cities, whether Urk or Babel. This is the immortality of civilization.

I will look at the relation between the technological man and his civilization through two of the oldest narratives about human origins:

a) the "humanization" of Enkidu found in *The Epic of Gilgamesh*; and

b) the expulsion from Paradise and the tower of Babel from the book of *Genesis*.

These stories seek to explain how we came to be the creatures we are. They are also stories that explain how the first cities were founded—and the connection between what we have lost (the garden) and what we have gained (civilization). We lost the garden and, *in its place*, we built the city. We have created machines that, through their spasmodic movements, imitate animal life. We need machines because we have lost the relationship we once had with animals. We are strangers in this garden from which we have been expelled, and we try to feel at home by building houses. Babylon was erected on the site of Eden; the *polis* is man's self-made paradise.

Upon his creation—from clay[36]—Enkidu knows no civilization:

> He knew neither people nor inhabited land,
> He dressed as animals do.
> He ate grass with gazelles,
> With beasts he jostled at the water hole,
> With wildlife drank his will of water.

He neither drinks wine (or, in his case, beer) nor eats cooked food. He wears no clothes and lives in the company of other wild animals with whom he has no need to

---

36   See, "Aruru wet her hands,
       She pinched off clay, she cast it down upon the steppe,
       She created valiant Enkidu in the steppe."

talk. We don't hear Enkidu talking until after his domestication by the harlot (Tablet I, line 223), and that only in order to express his consent to being admitted to the city and by extension to civilization. At this stage, he is only a "human-man," to borrow the translator's apt phrase that fits so well with the third etymology of Anthropos from *andros-opos*. He "turned into a man" however, only after he was dressed with clothes, had learned how to eat bread, drink beer and get drunk, and received a haircut. His transformation from human-looking animal to man proper and his initiation to civilization begins at the hands—or rather between the legs—of the harlot Shamhat. This might seem to you a little paradoxical, especially if you ask the question why is it through sex, one of the most animalistic of our desires and something we hold in common with them, that we gain admission to what is distinctively human, namely civilization? This kind of question presupposes the opposition between desire and civilization. It is true, *pace* Freud, that entry into the city requires submission to the law and repression of desire (and the challenge of channeling it elsewhere or otherwise), but that is a small price to pay for the overabundant compensation that the city, and our technological civilization, offers our desires in return. It is *willingly* that we submit to civilization because we are happy to exchange animal innocence for pleasure and convenience.[37]

Immediately after he has completed this intensive course in sex education, Enkidu has changed: his animal friends no longer recognize him and his animal strength has left him:

> When they saw him, Enkidu, the gazelles shied off,
> The wild beasts of the steppe shunned his person,

---

37   See, for example, how Socrates is detained at the beginning of the *Republic*.

Enkidu had polluted his virginal body.
His knees stood still, while his beasts were going away,
Enkidu was too slow, he could not run as before,
But he had gained [reason], broadened his understanding.

4. *De Genesi ad litteram*

Why is this? Why is it that through sex Enkidu gains knowledge? To answer this question, we need to turn to our second text (Gen. 3:1-13).

> Now the serpent was more subtle than any of the beasts of the earth which the Lord God had made. And he said to the woman: Why hath God commanded you, that you should not eat of every tree of paradise?
>
> 2 And the woman answered him, saying: Of the fruit of the trees that are in paradise we do eat:
>
> 3 But of the fruit of the tree which is in the midst of paradise, God hath commanded us that we should not eat; and that we should not touch it, lest perhaps we die.
>
> 4 And the serpent said to the woman: No, you shall not die the death.
>
> 5 For God doth know that in what day soever you shall eat thereof, your eyes shall be opened: and you shall be as Gods, knowing good and evil.
>
> 6 And the woman saw that the tree was good to eat, and fair to the eyes, and delightful to behold: and she took of the fruit thereof, and did eat, and gave to her husband who did eat.
>
> 7 And the eyes of them both were opened: and when they perceived themselves to be naked, they sewed together fig leaves, and made themselves aprons.
>
> 8 And when they heard the voice of the Lord God walking in paradise at the afternoon air, Adam and his wife hid them-

selves from the face of the Lord God, amidst the trees of paradise.

9 And the Lord God called Adam, and said to him: Where art thou?

10 And he said: I heard thy voice in paradise; and I was afraid, because I was naked, and I hid myself.

11 And he said to him: And who hath told thee that thou wast naked, but that thou hast eaten of the tree whereof I commanded thee that thou shouldst not eat?

12 And Adam said: The woman, whom thou gavest me to be my companion, gave me of the tree, and I did eat.

13 And the Lord God said to the woman: Why hast thou done this? And she answered: The serpent deceived me, and I did eat.

When we read that God planted a garden for Himself, we are to understand that the garden is this little blue and green planet of ours. We are still in the garden. We never left. It was, rather, something of the garden that was lost; or to be more precise, some characteristic of life in the garden as it was meant to be that has left us. As a result, our planetary garden has become as we know it—corruptible; and as it makes itself known to us—corrupted by us. The origin of the present-day environmental crisis lies with the fall. Now everything must be gained by *labor*—note how this is the common lot for both men and women, the one laboring at work, the other in birth—that is, by *effort*. The origin of work—not creation, which is recreational, but work that must be performed in order to sustain our life—lies also with the fall. Technology then—that is, the promise that technology makes to us, to restore the lost aspect of the garden and make it a paradise again and this time with the extra satisfaction of being a paradise made by us (not by Another)—comes also, albeit indirectly, from the fall, for technology is fallen man's attempt to undo the fall, that is, to lift himself up and become *Anthropos*. Notice how man falls when he stands up for himself, but rises when he falls, on his knees, in front of God.

"Now the serpent was more subtle than any of the beasts of the earth" (Gen. 3:1). The serpent is subtle like a lawyer, makes promises like a politician, and lies like both. The need for subtlety and the making of promises are, in and of themselves, enough to alert us that here we are dealing with seduction and deception; in a word: temptation. Nature makes no promises. The fruit up to now—that is, up to the moment that the serpent begins to make subtle distinctions about it—makes no promise, makes no claim, does not tempt anyone. Nature has no motive or intention beyond itself. Everything in nature exhausts itself in being itself. Now, however, when it is spoken of, *advertised*, now it appears *tempting* to the *eyes*.

The promise technology makes is this: *"[I]n what day soever you shall eat thereof, your eyes shall be opened: and you shall be as Gods, knowing good and evil."* (Gen. 3:5)

If one were able to go back and tell the most powerful men throughout history—be they Caesars, Czars, or Kaisers: people, in other words, who were worshiped like gods (and please note the comparison, these are men who have achieved what we all strive for: to become like gods)—if it were possible to go back in time and tell them that in our times one can have a warm home equipped with hot running water throughout the winter and a cool breeze in his bedchamber all summer long and do so *effortlessly*;[38] or the means to illuminate every corner of

---

38 This is of course the crucial word: *effortlessly*. For though it might have been possible to warm one's rooms in the past, it would require continuous effort and labor in constantly attending to the fire. Anyone today who has done so for sentimental reasons in front of a fireplace or a campfire, should know that

every room of his house *at will;* or to have any meal or drink his appetite might fancy delivered to his doorstep within the hour; or have his coffee made at the press of a button; or have the uncanny ability to summon in his presence the representations of absent people, whether living or dead, to hear them talk and talk with them as if they were present, and, in short, all of the other amenities modern technology makes possible to us, he would say that these were powers unfathomable to any earthly king, to be assigned perhaps only to a god, even if, as Freud aptly puts it, a *prosthetic* god. And if one were able to go back and tell King Solomon, in all his wisdom, that such god-like powers have been given to haughty rulers and to humble parlor maids equally, he would question whether our powerful devices have made the latter any happier or the former wiser than him.

Notice the emphasis on the eyes: "*And the woman* saw *that the tree was good to eat, and fair to the* eyes, *and delightful to* behold" (Gen. 3:6), and recall my example of the actor who, changing his appearance, could easily fool the eyes of his friends but not the nose of his dog, and you will understand why it was that our eyes deceived us. Do you now see why technology, as both the consequence of original sin and man's attempt to remake the garden he lost with his own artificial paradise, cannot but be *oculo-centric*? "*[A]nd she took of the fruit thereof, and did eat, and gave to her husband who did eat.*" (Gen. 3:6)

Nowadays there is a horrible saying that we have come to take for granted: 'A hungry stomach has no ears.' Well, at the time of which I speak, a stomach hungry for food and

---

maintaining a fire is not easy. I would have been a different person if I had been required to do that daily. I would have made different decisions in my life, if I had to do what people had to do daily in the past. In short, I would have been another, had I not been here now.

ears hungry for knowledge were one and the same thing, because the same fruits satisfied both hungers. Those fruits differed from ours not only in shape, color, and taste, but also in the knowledge they conferred. Some gave knowledge of plants and animals and others of mathematics; there was a geography fruit, a music fruit, and many more. And to those who ate of them, they imparted, along with this knowledge, the corresponding virtues: courage to sailors, gentleness to surgeon-barbers, honesty to historians, faith to theologians, devotion to physicians, patience to teachers. In those days man shared in the divine simplicity. Body and soul were molded of the same substance. The mouth was a living temple—draped in purple, with its double semicircle of enamel footstools, its fonts of saliva and its nasal chimneys, with its word that nourishes and its food that teaches, its truth that is food and drink, and its fruits that melt into ideas, precepts, and axioms.[39]

There is a decisive change that takes place when man falls, as decisive as the passage from nothing into everything that took place at the creation of the world. This very world has turned upside-down and inside-out. Everything becomes distorted. For to eat from the fruit of the tree of the knowledge of good and evil is to know good as evil (and to mistake evil for good).

The nature of the Fall—both while possible and when actual—is clearly defined. The 'fruit of the tree' is to bring an increase of knowledge. That increase, however, is, and is desired as being, of a particular kind. It is not merely to know more, but to know in another method. It is primarily the advance (if it can be so called) from knowing good to knowing good and evil; it is (secondarily) the knowing 'as gods:' A certain knowledge was, by its nature, confined to divine being. Its communication to man would be, by its

---

39 Michel Tournier, *The Four Wise Men*, translated by Ralph Manheim (Baltimore: The Johns Hopkins University Press, 1997), p. 178.

> nature, disastrous to man. . . . It is easy for us now, after the terrible and prolonged habit of mankind; it was not, perhaps, very difficult then—as easy as picking a fruit from a tree. It was merely to wish to know an antagonism in the good, to find out what the good would be like if a contradiction were introduced into it. Man desired to know schism in the universe. . . . The contradiction in the nature of man is thus completely established, He knows good, and he knows good as evil These two capacities will always be present in him; his love will always be twisted with anti-love, with anger, with spite, with jealousy, with alien desires.[40]

That fruit was sweet in the mouth but bitter in the stomach. It appeared desirable but it was deadly. Among the other results of the Fall one should also include the separation between being and appearance, the possibility of conceit, and the actuality of the lie.

The fall of man broke the truth into two pieces: an empty, hollow, false word without nutritive value, and a compact, heavy, opaque, and greasy food, which beclouds the spirit and is converted into paunches and double chins.

> [H]umanity itself, being the imago Dei, is majestic. But since when we lost our innocence at the Fall, we lost also our freedom to wear the real robe of our majesty, namely, our nakedness, we have now to try to remember and acknowledge that majesty by second-best tokens like crowns and scepters and gold. These say as best they can, 'Behold the glory of man.'[41]

---

40 Charles Williams, "The Myth of the Alteration in Knowledge" in *He Came Down from Heaven* (Berkeley, CA: The Apocryphile Press, 2005), pp. 19-22.

41 Thomas Howard, *The Novels of Charles Williams* (Eugene, Oregon: Wipf & Stock, 2004), pp. 62-3.

5. Gymnopedia: Language and Nudity

Let us consider the creation of clothing in the *Genesis* narrative: "And the *eyes* of them both were *opened*: and when they perceived themselves to be *naked*, they sewed together fig leaves, and made themselves aprons" (Gen. 3:7). A few lines later, Adam says, "because I was naked, I hid myself" (Gen. 3:10). Standing up reveals one's belly and what used to be called one's privates (when they were still private); the orthograde position exposes one's underbelly: to all animals it is a position of shame and vulnerability—a very private side that an animal would never show to another but reserves only for those it trusts and as a sign of their trust and intimacy.

> Besides, the dog that stands on two hind legs exhibits his privates most brazenly, like man, and most cynically, as they say. The dog does just what man did when he first stood up and became a vertical mammal, and immediately felt shame, because he was soon covering his exposed parts. I've heard that their Bible tells them that the first man, that is, the first of them who began to walk about on two legs, was ashamed to appear naked before his God. So they invented clothing, to cover their sex. . . . Those pants of theirs are a simple consequence of standing up on their hind legs. And what a strange beast he is, man! His mind is never where it should be, that is, it's never on what he's doing. And he talks in order to lie. And he puts on clothes![42]

The speaker of this passaged is an authority on the subject, for he is himself a dog named Orfeo in Unamuno's nivola *Mist* (also translated as *Fog*).

If we don't feel shame or if we humans take the risk to expose our underbellies to everyone we meet, that is

---

[42] Miguel de Unamuno, *Mist*, in *Selected Works of Migue de Unamuno*, volume 6: *Novela/Nivola* (Princeton: Princeton University Press, 1976), p. 244.

because we have an ace of another kind up our sleeves: we can stand up and expose ourselves because we are covered first by our clothes and secondly by our language (notice how language and clothes appear together and at the same time as a result of the Fall). Even if nude, humans are never completely naked as long as they can hide behind language. As the clothes hide the body while at the same time revealing the style or the function—think of vesture, costume, uniforms and of how many distinctions are conveyed and communicated by articles of clothing—so language, and ultimately reflection, hide our inner thoughts, while at the same time revealing and expressing our character. The hiding is twofold (hiding of body and of mind) because dualism is founded upon duplicity. It is the lie (what Plato calls the *true lie*) that creates interiority and inwardness and, thus, the need to exteriorize what is intimate and express what lies inside.

From what I judge by looking around, most of you don't even have a theory of dressing; you probably wear something because it is convenient or because you think it makes you look a certain way. I believe a man should have a theory behind his dress—for as one dresses, so he thinks—and institute a dress code for himself with the same consideration that he would have given in deciding a uniform or a habit for a new order. Naturally, you would feel rather vulnerable, if I could see behind your clothes, but you would feel even more naked and exposed, if I could read your mind. The *naked* truth, we say—truth allegorized in paintings is also represented as a nude figure—because clothes lie.[43]

---

43 On the important subject of clothes, and their philosophical rapport, I recommend the unsurpassable *Sartor Resartus* by Thomas Carlyle. A book to be read at least once by anyone who wears clothes.

"And Adam said: The woman, whom thou gavest me to be my companion, gave me of the tree, and I did eat. And the Lord God said to the woman: Why hast thou done this? And she answered: The serpent deceived me, and I did eat" (Gen. 3:11-12). As soon they can speak, which is as soon as they see that they are naked, they lie.

> Adam's one task in the Garden had been to invent language, to give each creature and thing its name. In the state of innocence, his tongue had gone straight to the quick of the world. His words had not been merely appended to things he saw, they had revealed their essences, had literally brought them to life. A thing and its name were interchangeable. After the fall, this was no longer true. Names became detached from things; words devolved into a collection of arbitrary signs; language had been severed from God. The story of the Garden, therefore, records not only the fall of man, but the fall of language.[44]

There is something innately artificial about language. There is something unnatural in the speaking animal. Animals speak only in fables and fairy tales, not in reality. If Orfeo spoke the words we quoted above, that was in order to give his late master, Augusto Pérez, one of the most profound eulogies offered at a funeral.

My cat was not willing to wait until such a time. He slunk out of his leather carrier and with a single jump he mounted the lectern. Michael, named so after the Archangel of Death, was one of those intelligent black cats who somehow found it necessary to interrupt me in order to make a comment on a subject that apparently was dear to him, for I had no idea he had so much to say.

----

44 Paul Auster, *City of Glass*, (Penguin Books, 1985), p. 70.

6. The Extempore Catechesis of Michael the Archangelic Cat

"The human animal," *said Michael*, "is the animal that calls itself an animal. Man is the animal that says 'I am an animal'—which is something that no other animal does and therefore it sets man apart from the rest of us, his animal siblings. Why does the human animal speak? Isn't it this curious? Doesn't it sound suspicious that one among all the other animals speaks and says, 'I am an animal'? Maybe it is precisely the animal that says 'I am an animal' that is *not* an animal at all. He speaks in order to lie. As he speaks so he lies.[45]

"The speaking mouth is, from the very first moment, the lying mouth, for in language the *saying* takes the place of the *showing* or of the *doing*, which is how we animals communicate. But to say it without having to show

---

45 What is *dolus* as opposed to a mere lie? *Dolus* is not a lie in words but a lie of character. It is the frame of mind that subjugates every act of will and willful action to one end: to create a *pose* and to pose as someone other than your true self. Dolus is to aim at making an impression, to seek someone's attention, to assume a studied posture, to speak in borrowed expressions. All the modalities of our everyday life operate on *dolus*. The anchorite and the hermit who retreat to the desert, they do so in order to remove or at least eliminate as much as possible the occasion and opportunity for *dolus*. The characteristic trait of the saint is, first and foremost, a conduct free of *dolus*. *Dolus* is exclusively a symptom of the City—it exists only in life within the *polis*, and it is best seen as the prevailing ethos of politics. It is a political sin. *Dolus* is the world of news and newspapers, of social media, of corporate policies and of academic administrators. Notice how in the Psalms one always meets *dolus* in public squares, holding hands with usury: καὶ οὐκ ἐξέλιπεν ἐκ τῶν πλατειῶν αὐτῆς τόκος καὶ δόλος/*et non defecit de plateis ejus usura et dolus*. (Ps. 54 [55]:11 [12]). I have made the same point in the Second of my *Fenwick Essays* on the occasion of discussing the anthropology of the Psalmist.

it, without having to do it—hence, only in *words*, not in deeds, as the distinction goes—is to lie.

"A cat cannot speak. I cannot say: 'I would like to have my dinner served now please,' but when my bowl is empty, or very nearly empty, I *show* it by standing by it as if to say, 'Here I am and the bowl is here, there is only one thing missing, the food. Please put my food into the bowl.' A dog is not able to say, 'Let's go for a walk,' but does he communicate it any less clearly when he stands by the door with his leash in his mouth? It is very strange to us animals when we hear you say, "I'm going" while you remain seated, precisely as theatergoers feel when they hear the characters in Beckett's *Waiting for Godot* talking without acting. There is a remaining absurdity on the foundation of language as such insofar as the saying is not the said, and the signifier is not the thing thereby signified.

"It was by language that human beings domesticated the unpredictable and unstable great outdoors, that is, the real. The domesticating *domus* has something to do with it. The house is, first and foremost, as the German Master, Heidegger, said, the house of *language*. Before man rose from the ground, and as if it were a monument to *homo erectus*, he began to erect houses from the ground up, as opposed to finding shelter in and within the ground as his cave-dwelling relatives did. 'Let us make a name,' said the builders of the Tower of Babel. Their name would have been the walls of Babel. The laws of the city are like the walls of the *polis* (says Heraclitus) and the *nomen* of Babel's is its *nomos*, and in this common derivation the connection between building and language is already suggested. The distinction between an inside and an outside, their non-coincidence on which language dwells, that is the possibility of lying, becomes the condition of privacy for it becomes externalized and materialized in the walls of the house. Before the first human built the first house, there was no *inside* in things: everything was out there, in the open. There isn't even outdoors, strictly speaking, until there is an indoors. The distinction between an inside and an outside, and the distinction between private and public, originate with the walls of the first house. Yet it is *language* that first introduces the distinction between in/out, the distinction which is the result of the difference between the said and the saying, upon which then the House is founded as a memorial that embodies the division of language.

"An animal knows the difference: outside everything moves and grows and nothing remains the same. Even when this change becomes constant and periodic—as in the cycle of days and seasons—the variations are as infinite as the variables and their endless combinations. Take the light, for example, at any given day or hour of the day as it is constantly changed not only by the position of the sun to the earth, but also by a myriad of other factors, such as the location and its proximity to mountains or the sea, its elevation, the atmospheric pressure of the day and number of other aerial phenomena that interplay with the quality of the light (clouds, mists, fogs), and so on. Indoors, however, everything remains as static as possible. It is a *controlled* environment. Outside things grow and change constantly. There is not a single moment that is identical to another, and it is against such Heraclitean impermanence that humans erect the walls of their houses within which they can achieve an Eleatic constancy. Inside the house, nothing changes and everything is already dead.

"Similarly, language lent its own fixity to an unstable world that is, after Heraclitus, in continuous flux. The word 'fire,' for example, is always the same, made of the same four letters, but the reality to which this word refers, the burning fire, is not. I have sat many nights by the fireplace mesmerized by the ever-changing flames, not one similar to all the others even to the acuity of my feline eyesight. By having the word, man can forego the anxiety that impermanence induces, for the permanent word allows him to pretend that the impermanent world is made up by things as speech is made up by words (and that things are like words, permanent). To *pretend*, I say: it is a pretention of reality. And so, you have the following genealogy of lies: the lie of original sin (to man's self-gazing eye, each appears two) begets the lie of language ('this is a pipe' can be said of any 'pipe') and that, in turn, engenders the epistemological lie of the real, that is, of a reality divided between itself and its other. It was best said by a dog—don't be surprised—that same Orfeo, who once remarked:

> But he barks in his own special way, in any case, that's his talk, and he's used it to invent things that don't exist, forgetting to pay attention to what does exist. As soon as he can find a name for something, he forgets about it, he can't even see it. He's happy just to hear the name of the thing or to see it written down. His language is good for lying, for inventing whatever isn't, and for getting everything confused.[46]

"Suppose a cat is caught in the rain—I won't lie, it has happened to me. Do you think that I have a concept of that? Think rather more of a *strategy* encoded in a sequence of movements, like a dance, in response to the situation 'getting-caught-in-the-rain.' And it is incumbent upon any cat that he should follow them accurately and practice them assiduously precisely as a pianist must follow the rules of position and figuration in response to

---

46   Miguel de Unamuno, *Mist*, in *Selected Works of Migue de Unamuno*, volume 6: *Novela/Nivola* (Princeton: Princeton University Press, 1976), p. 242.

any situation his keyboard might present him with. It is therefore a cat's virtue to become a virtuoso in applying and adapting his skills to his environment. But because a human being has *concepts*, he is by far less adept in responding to his environment. He—the human—would rather have the environment submit to his concepts: and so, he builds his house (and houses make up cities, as cities make up civilizations).

"The House fulfils the human need for a clear distinction between the controlled environment of the indoors over the outdoors which human beings cannot control and where ants and bugs crawl about all the time. Could you please tell me, what instinct and what fear compels you to kill the ant on the kitchen floor? It poses no threat to you and does no damage—if anything it cleans the floor of crumbs. It might not pose a threat to you, but it does to your *arrangement* and that's equally or perhaps even more of a threat to you, for it turns things inside-out. The ant on the kitchen floor, the spider over the bookshelves, the dead bird I brought my human once—they pose no danger to you except that their presence *there where they have been banned by you* (namely, the house) violates a boundary and contaminates the stillness of life indoors, controlled and regulated by you, with the unpredictability of the outdoors.

"Notice how the comfort of the house, that is its homeliness, derives from and depends upon its being a space that is controlled and regulated by you, a space where *you* are in control and were *you* make the rules. 'My roof, my rules,' as parents like to say (an echo of Heraclitus 'the laws of the city are as its walls,' the builder of the wall is the giver of the law). It is an illusion of course, for it operates by a distinction that is itself based on an illusion. There aren't any more 'indoors' in the house than there is in your mind: everything takes place outside. It was only after man's fall that he became hallowed, that his body was not him but *his*, like the shell of a tortoise, in which he lives hidden from the eyes and minds of others.

"Once expelled from Paradise, language became concrete in building first the House and then the City as, inside Paradise, but immediately after the Fall, language makes itself visible in the clothes your ancestors made for themselves in order to cover their newly discovered nakedness. The connection between man's ability to speak and to build is epitomized in the story of the tower of Babel. To stop them from building, God confused their language. When language fails to do what language aims at doing (to wit, to communicate what is inside to those who are outside), so does man's ability to build walls that distinguish indoors from outdoors. That knowledge, of which you are all so proud, is a substitute for that innocence which you lost but that is still preserved in us animals. If we, animals, neither speak nor put on clothes, that's because we didn't fall. Yet, to the extent that we too are part of God's creation, we shared in the punishment of your actions and so, together with you, we die even though we didn't sin.

~*~*~

Thus spoke Michael the Cat who exited the stage of the lecture hall as suddenly and elegantly as he had entered it. After a few silent moments of reflection during which we tried to take in all the points of the Cat's discourse, I continued:

I believe that Michael spoke surprisingly well. Perhaps others would say that what was surprising is that he spoke at all. Yet, if God opened the mouth of a donkey in order to preach to the prophet Balaam (Numbers, 22:21-34), I don't see why a cat, especially such a well-read cat as mine, could not lecture a room of scholars and scholastics.

When man regains an approximation of that Paradisiac state that we lost, he has no use of either knowledge or language: the saint in his mystical vision, for example, or the fool in his foolishness; whether high—as high as Paul in his heavenward flight in the 1st Corinthians 13:8-9: "whether there be tongues, they shall cease; whether there be knowledge, it shall vanish away, for we know in part . . . but when that which is perfect is come, then that which is in part shall be done away"—or low, as low as Bottom's bottomless dream: "Methought I was—there is no man can tell what. Methought I was, and methought I had—but man is but a patch'ed fool, if he will offer to say what methought I had. The eye of man hath not heard, the ear of man hath not seen, man's hand is not able to taste, his tongue to conceive, nor his heart to report, what my dream was" (*A Midsummer's Night Dream*, act IV, scene 1).

7. Auto-Eidolon

It is essential to remind us that our word *idol* is a relative of the Greek word for a mirror: *eidolon.* From first to last, all idols are mirror-images, and this *mirroring*, this similitude, *makes* you that which you worship. You become your idol, but in the sense of the Psalmic verse: "Those who make them [the idols] will be like them and so will all who trust in them" (Ps. 113:16 [115:8] and Ps. 134:18 [135:18]).

I return to Genesis 3:7, "And the eyes of them both were opened: and they perceived themselves to be naked." Not only, however, did they see themselves naked, they also *saw themselves*—and that is by far the more decisive vision. The most basic facts of life—birth and death—

elude us. The bare minimum of any biography is the time and place of birth and the time and manner of death of a person: Where was he born, to which parents, and when did he die and how? These are the very facts that we neither control nor remember. We do not experience being born and have no memory of it at all. What we know is what we have been told *by others*. It is as if we ourselves were not even there. We don't choose our parents, our country, our station in life. When we are born, we find ourselves already determined by all these factors and more. It is as if we are actors given our parts and we now find out whether we will be king or beggar, villain or hero. We are characters in a story that has begun long before us—except that, unlike actors, we don't have the script in advance. We have to play ourselves and, in so doing, discover who we are supposed to be in the plot of our lives.

"And the eyes of them both were opened: and they perceived themselves." For the first time, man *notices* himself. That is tremendous. A momentous movement has taken place by turning away from God (from the One, as Plotinus would say)—and he must be turning away from God if he turns his attention upon himself, for he *notices* himself—and since, by the *narrowness of consciousness*, as Husserl calls it, attention can be only at *one* place at each given moment, since, that is, consciousness can have only *one* object at a time, for consciousness can see only what it illuminates like a spotlight, once the spotlight of attention has turned upon itself, it cannot be on God any longer. And yet, if man turns away from God because he turns towards himself, he turns away from the One and in so doing becomes *many*. Indeed, we become many by first becoming two: for by turning our attention upon ourselves, by becoming self-regarding, we have made ourselves into an Object. Self-regard is self-objectifying. Man becomes a Subject by making himself an Object first; for there is an object only for a subject and by virtue of a subject. It is the objectifying regard that constitutes the self-regarding self. I am talking of an original self-objectification (itself the consequence of self-regard, αὐταρέσεκεια), back to which one must date the origins of consciousness, and thus the origins of humanity. It was then that man was split in two.

Something of tremendous importance happens when Man turns his objectifying gaze—now that he has looked up—and his abstracting language—now that he speaks and is spoken—upon himself. He conceives (of) himself, his self, and says "I": an I that would come to claim body and mind as his; "my body," he says and "my ideas." He puts his name on everything: "his" pleasure and "his" pain—his *proper* name: the birth of *property*. At the same time, an entirely new dimension, or direction, in space opens up, a new spatial category is created: *the indoors*. I am now convinced that the inside/outside distinction is based on the interiority created by sin or, to use Luther's Latin *cor curvum in se*—and not the other way around. The recesses of the mind (Montaigne's back room)[47] predate those of our houses. Man, I believe, builds his house in imitation of his soul. Because he is aware of that space of interiority where he goes to hide from the scrutiny of the Other's gaze, now that he hides from the Other's face, he seeks to recreate, without, with bricks and mortar, the very distinction between an inside and an outside which he has first experienced within. The house is a monument that commemorates and marks (re-enacts) this distinction. The threshold is a border (protected, as it is today, by law) that separates not only the inside from the out-

---

47 Montaigne, *On Solitude*: "We must reserve a room all our own behind the store, completely free, in which we establish our true liberty, our main retreat and solitude."

side, the private from the public, but also the natural (the outdoors) from the artificial, and the human from the non-human.

Now that man has learned to love an object, in taking himself as his loving object, his desire is turned toward objects in general which can represent to him that quality which he loves in himself. Desire is for the mind what weight is for bodies, says St. Augustine, and the law of attraction is as inexorable as the law of gravity, for it binds you to your object of desire and makes you like it.

> Holy things were profaned when mankind made its grab for power and knowledge in Eden, saying, 'This shall be ours', and the unity was ripped. Not, of course, the Unity of Godhead itself but the unity that bound all creation, both matter and spirit, into one seamless pattern. Thereafter, we were doomed to experience things as divided: profane and sacred, matter and spirit, mortal and immortal, visible and invisible.[48]

---

48 Thomas Howard, *The Novels of Charles Williams* (Eugene, Oregon: Wipf & Stock, 2004), p. 121.

At the Sext

(That is, around noon)

"But Saint Gregory says that Adam broke the commandment at the Sext hour."[49]

To resume our discussion, let us ask: What *kind* of technology does fallen man create? The first characteristic, as we have seen already, is that it is oculocentric. It couldn't have been otherwise since this is the product of Anthropos—the one who looks up, who is thus defined by his ability to look. Man's ability to see (*theoria*) liberates his hand, or rather, elevates the hand from being one of the feet of the quadrupedal animal into the *function* of handling (*praxis*). Moving from *theoria* to *praxis* we arrived next at *logos*, for the foot has been elevated to the dignity of the hand (and remember what Heidegger says, only man has a hand) and has opened up the world of *praxis*, that is, the practical world, thereby liberating the mouth which once performed the rudimentary functions of handling. Only when the mouth ceases to act as a hand is it free to *speak*.

This is the outline of our discussion so far. There is, however, another characteristic of fallen man that perhaps has something to do with another function of the human body, in common with other animals, but perhaps all the more dangerous when, such an animal ability falls into the hands of fallen man who can technologically machinate it: the ability to move. It would have been a

---

49   Bob Miller, "A Dutch Translation of The Life of Adam and Eve" in *Ons Geestelijk Erf* 80(4), 313-373, at 342.

different story if man was like a tree firmly planted in the soil from which he came. I very much doubt whether such rooted men would have come up with the notion of free will or whether they would have believed, as we now do, in the illusion of independence. As it is, man is now an upside-down tree, with his bulb-head up in the air, moving on the face of the earth with his feet as some other animals move on the bottom of the sea with their tentacles. There was a time, Aristophanes says in Plato's *Symposium*, that men could run even faster (ταχὺ ὁρμή- σειεν θεῖν, 190a5); it was perhaps because of their ability to move that they turned against the gods. "Our power of locomotion is an enemy to religion," writes Chapman and I think he is right.

8. Art and Creation

You remember, of course, that in Aristophanes' little tragicomedy, there were three kinds of creatures. Well, so too in today's lecture will we distinguish three catego- ries or classes of creation:

a)   a being who creates but is not created—the Creator;
b)   a being which is created and cannot itself create—Creation;
c)   and, finally, a being who is both creature and creator—*Anthropos*.

While God creates not only the form but, together with the form, the matter out of which creation is brought into existence, man can create only by re-creating, that is, by rearranging matter and combing the forms that are already *given* to us by our Creator. Strictly speaking, we neither invent anything nor create anything new. All our creativity consists in taking what we have been given and changing it into something else. For example, a fish and a woman are both creatures within God's creation. Man may think that he created something new by coming up with the idea of a mermaid, or a centaur, or a sphinx—creatures that presumably don't exist in God's creation—but all he has done is combine pre-existing forms and re-arrange pre-existing matter. Here, then, we have discovered a more fundamental distinction: God's creation is original, in the sense that it borrows nothing, while human creation is secondary, in the sense that it depends formally and materially on God's creation.

Nevertheless, re-creation is a fitting name for human creativity, for man's art and artistry are truly *recreational*: by creating, man recreates himself. To take what is given and change it is to transform it in a way that now bears something of you on it, it bears the stamp of your character—what in art we call *style*. Style is unmistakable both in painting and in music. You cannot mistake a composition by Mozart or a painting by van Gogh for something else. Then the question arises: *Where is style?*

> *Is it in the colors*? But these are the same colors that all other painters have used.
> *Is it in the brushstroke?* All painters use some kind of brush.
> *Is it in the canvass?*

It is none of these and all of them together and then—something *more*. Yes, there were sunflowers in the world before van Gogh, but van Gogh's sunflowers can't be found anywhere else.

9. Creation and Procreation

If all life is generative, human life alone is also creative. Or, to put it in the language of the discussion to come, not only can man self-generate (as in formal reproduction, where individuals of a species reproduce themselves and, through them, their species), but he can also create, that is, he can generate what is other-than-himself.

However, whatever other-than-ourselves we are able to create must be other-than-ourselves in another fundamental sense: it can never be, like us, *living*. Here is then the fundamental restriction, and perhaps even the fundamental frustration, of human creativity: as long as man's image is the same (that is, another human) man can create life, but as soon as man's image is other than man, it must be different from him in this way: it will *not* be alive. In the end, we are left with two distinct possibilities: on the one hand, we have the ability to procreate, and the offspring of procreation will be like ourselves, "in our image and likeness," and also, like ourselves, living, and, on the other hand, we have the ability to create, and the offspring of creation will be *not* like ourselves and *not* living.

What God creates grows (it is this "growing" that lies behind our philosophical concepts of *physis* and *physics* > φύω): God creates a tree and the tree grows and it will keep growing for many summers and winters and until other trees come from it, and they too will continue to grow and multiply. To whatever God has created He has imparted the power of life, a *vitality* proper to its own (this is true even for what we take to be inanimate matter) which the "Book of Generations," called *Genesis*, indicates by the formula "grow and multiply" (or "be fruitful and multiply": Gen. 1:22, 28). When Man, however, makes a table out of that same tree, the table *neither* grows *nor* multiplies.

Now, if we look closely at the two distinct possibilities of human creativity that we have described so far, namely the ability to procreate and the ability to recreate, we will begin to suspect that their essential difference—that the former generates a living image of ourselves, while the latter reproduces a non-living image of something other than ourselves—is itself based on the difference between primary and secondary creation. If man cannot create life that is because he is himself a creature and his inability to master life is proof of his creaturely being.

10. Until Now

For as soon as the machines we made became alive . . .

The idea that machines can learn is scarcely surprising in the world of artificial intelligence; that not only they learn, but they also adapt and respond to our behavioral and thinking patterns is proven daily by our smart phones; that in doing so they determine our perception of ourselves and our reality we now begin slowly to realize—but to call them *living*? Life is of course a phenomenon notoriously difficult to define—but if machines reproduce, interact, adapt, respond, and communicate what do we call them? And, more importantly, what do we call ourselves who created them?

In his *New Babel* (published in 1690 in Cambridge, Massachusetts), Henry Dark made the prediction that it is the New Babel, namely the New World newly settled by the pilgrims of Mayflower fame, that will fulfill the mission of the old Tower, not only by being the only nation on God's earth to build skyscrapers, but by making man truly like a God and giving him all of God's other attributes, not just heavenward heights: omniscience, omnipresence and, finally, immortality. Dark's prediction came with a calculation and an explanation. "Just as Babel had been built 340 years after the Flood, so it would be, Dark predicted, exactly 340 years after the arrival of the Mayflower at Plymouth that the commandment would be carried out."[50] If you begin counting from 1620, the date of Mayflower's arrival in Plymouth, that would bring us up to 1960; others, however, have supported that the 340 years should be counted beginning with the date of the publication of Dark's prophecy, that is with 1690; thus their calculations reach the year 2030. In any case, something happened between 1960 and 2030 that has made man into a prosthetic God.

11. God & Golem, Inc.

Some twenty years ago, I happened to find shelter from a rainy day in one of our city's excellent bookstores that trade old and antiquarian books.[51] Among them I found a small book in a black cover with red and white letters: the author was a certain Norbert Wiener and the title read *God & Golem, Inc.* At first it seemed to me to be one of those self-published pamphlets that, having left their author's basements, can reach all philosophy departments around the nation, on the conviction that the as-of-yet-unthought ideas that they communicate to mankind would bestow a modest measure of glory upon their authors. Only this was not published in a basement but by M.I.T. Press in 1964. The copy I had in my hands was the sixth printing of 1985. It had won the National Book Award.

---

50   Paul Auster, *City of Glass*, p. 78.
51   It was the old *Commonwealth Books*, when it was located in Boylston St., across the commons, and a few yards from Edgar Allan Poe's house. I returned to the same place a couple years later with Jean-Luc Marion who found two volumes of St. Basil's letters printed with facing Greek and French. It was this gift that later became the foundation for my essay on "Friendship in Late Antiquity"—which I consider to be one of the best things I have written. But I digress.

Norbert Wiener, hailed as the father of automation and cybernetics, was a professor of mathematics at M.I.T. for forty years, having first astonished the world with his career as a prodigy child: he graduated from high school at the age of 11 and from Tufts College, with a B.A. in mathematics, at age 14; he went on to study zoology at Harvard and philosophy at Cornell with Bertrand Russell; he received his Ph.D. from Harvard at 19 years old.[52] In his last book he makes the wild claim that man has become, *like God*, able to create a *living* operative image of himself. By the end of this little book, the claim is no longer left implicit, but stated in all its creative force:

> The machine, as I have already said, is the modern counterpart of the Golem of the Rabbi of Prague. Since I have insisted upon discussing creative activity under one heading, and in not parceling it out into separate pieces belonging to God, to man, and to the machine, I do not consider that I have taken more than an author's normal liberty in calling this book *GOD AND GOLLEM, Inc.*

The idea that reproduction in living organisms must be thought of as being analogous to a process of reproduction in machines was suggested to him by what he had observed in its nascent state, namely the ability of a machine to learn. Learning, however, as he rightly observes "is a property that we often attribute exclusively to self-conscious systems, and almost always to living systems." A "game-playing machine," for example, "will continually transform itself into a different machine, in accordance with the history of the actual play." And he continues:

> In playing against such a machine, which absorbs part of its playing personality from its opponent, this playing per-

---

52 I cite his obituary in *New York Times*, March 19, 1964: "Dr. Norbert Wiener, Dead at 69, Known as Father of Automation."

sonality will not be absolutely rigid. The opponent may find
that stratagems which have worked in the past, will fail to
work in the future. The machine may develop an uncanny
canniness.

Such uncanny canniness, however, is the result not only
of the interaction between the machine and its program-
mer or its user; a machine can learn from other machines
with which it is "related" by a heredity of *operative
images*. The latter is another of Wiener's own concepts
which he coined in order to distinguish between pictorial and operative images. As my father's son, I am both
his pictorial and operative image in the sense that in me
is reproduced a likeness of him (as modified by generic
variation), yet a likeness that is not only an image that
looks like him (pictorial), but also an image that is also
capable of performing the same functions as he, for I am
another living human being (operative likeness). A statue
of myself—should one be erected on the campus of Holy
Cross or, dare I say, your illustrious campus—would be a
pictorial image but not an operative one (unless it is one
of those *speaking* statues of Memnon). While a machine,
capable of copying and performing some of my capacities, is not a pictorial image but can be taken to be an
operative image of me or at least of the capacity that it
has learned to perform. And the machine that reproduces
itself (that is, its abilities) in other machines, passing to
them its own learning, is even more so. Wiener had anticipated a time when "the machine may generate the message, and the message may generate another machine."
The generated machines are related to their originals as
operative copies to their archetypes and the very line of
generation through which they evolve and develop should
be thought, Wiener argues, as mechanical reproduction.

It is a claim that has become a warning too: the Golem,
to which Wiener is here referring, is the creature made by

the famous Maharal of Prague, Rabbi Löw, who, in an act that echoes God's creation of man in *Genesis*, fashioned a creature out of clay which he was then able to animate with the kabbalistic power of three Hebrew letters— *aleph, mem, tav*—that spell the word אמת (*'emét,* Hebrew for "truth") that was inscribed upon it. When things turn awry, as they always do in such stories, the Rabbi is able to deactivate the creature, as if by turning off a switch, simply by erasing the first letter of the word which now spells מת (*mét,* Hebrew for "dead"). Here you have *techne* (the fashion of clay into an anthropomorphic statue) and *logos* (the written word, the "code" that animates it), that is, technology; but here you also have something else: a spell—that is, *magic.*

12. Magic and the Machine

The comparison of machine to Golem is an appropriate one: *magic* and the *machine,* after all, have the same root—and not only linguistically. Their operation and their objectives are also the same: power(s) put in the service of (effortless: i.e., automatic) pleasure motivated by greed (Simony) and curiosity (Sorcery). It might be true that the mechanical is derived from the magical, as astronomy originates in astrology and chemistry in alchemy. The comparison of the one to the other, however, goes deeper than the etymologies of the words and the genealogy of ideas, as Wiener makes clear:

> There is a sin, which consists of using the magic of modern automatization to further personal profit or let loose the apocalyptic terrors of nuclear warfare. If this sin is to have a name, let that name be Simony or Sorcery.

And first, with respect to the motive of Simony, that is, the exploitation of supernatural, be it divine or mechanical:

> Once such a master becomes aware that some of the sup-
> posedly human functions of his slaves may be transferred
> to machines, he is delighted. At last he has found the new
> subordinate—efficient, subservient, dependable in his
> action, never talking back, swift, and not demanding a sin-
> gle thought of personal consideration.

And also, cheap. Now he can dispense altogether with the human slaves, the employees and their wages.

But also, dangerous, as dangerous as black magic. W. W. Jacobs' macabre story of "The Monkey's Paw" is then recalled in order to make precisely this point:

> [T]he operation of magic is singularly literal-minded, and
> that if it grants you anything at all it grants what you ask
> for, not what you should asked for or what you intend. . . .
> The magic of automation, and in particular the magic of an
> automatization in which the devices learn, may be expected
> to be similarly literal-minded.

A warning that has become infinitely more relevant on the wake of artificial intelligence. Take, for example, the case of the Soviet lieutenant Stanislav Petrov who, on September 26th, 1983, "saved the world" when he decided to disregard an early warning that the nuclear detection system had issued claiming that a nuclear mis-sile had been launched by the US followed by five more. He, Stanislav Petrov, decided not to initiate a retaliatory response, as he was supposed to, according to military protocols, judging what subsequent investigation proved to be correct that the warning system had malfunctioned. Had he acted as any intelligent Golem would have in his place—for they are specifically designed to follow proto-cols—I would not be speaking these words now. The vir-tue of human "intelligence" lies precisely in our capacity to *disobey* protocols of action.

Not all catastrophes, however, are as apocalyptic as nuclear annihilation. And some of the worst catastrophes are imperceptible. There was a time, for example, when in order to find their way, whether walking or driving, people would rely on landmarks and mental associations. It was of course possible to get lost, and one often did, but getting lost is the best way to find your way around. And that's the problem with technology: one cannot get lost anymore—thanks to our devices, we will always find our way without effort and without pain.

Yet it is with great effort and pain that all intellectual and spiritual goods are acquired. The magic of technology is that it achieves things *as if* by a divine *fiat*: that is, effortlessly. Throughout history and up to the last century, everything that man wanted and needed done took effort. In the advent of industrial and technological revolutions, effort was replaced by money. Now everything man wants and needs done takes money. The substitution of effort with money produces a world that values comfort over virtue (which is acquired with effort) and defines success, not on the basis of achievement and merit, but exclusively on material possessions. However, the joy of possession consists in being, so to speak, the *reward* for one's efforts and, therefore, an effortless possession cannot but become quickly joyless, as a comfortable lifestyle becomes quickly boring. Thus, one is left with no other distraction but self-destructive vice and addiction.

On the basis of what has been said up to now, it is safe, I believe, to assume that we are confronted not with a new challenge, but with the newest apparition of our oldest enemy. I think we can call it our *Golem* and describe it as that configuration of human life according to a series of new capabilities made possible by digital technology. Every aspect of the world and all expressions of human life in the world have been transfigured by technology, from Church services to dating, from Banks to factories, from Colleges and Universities to States and Governments. And the changes are not anymore only peripheral and external, as was the difference that the world underwent on the wake of industrialization, but essential: the difference between illuminating a building by gas-light or by electric bulbs leaves the building in question much the same, but when the functions of the building are separated and removed from it so that its location makes no difference anymore and its physical material (walls, roofs, staircases) are not needed any more, that building is not the same. In fact, nothing is the same anymore. And the question becomes: What are we to do? Is there anything that can be done or have we lost this war before we even had a chance to fight it?

At the None

(That is, around 3:00 p.m.)

"According to Spanish folklore the Last Judgement is to occur at three o'clock in the afternoon, the hour of Christ's death on the Cross."[53]

Now "as fades the day's last light and we see the lamps of night"—let me ask you: Do you believe that light is still there even when we have closed our eyes? That honey is still sweet even if no tongue is tasting it? Even though one understands that both light and sweetness are sensations and that sensation, understood properly, is not a property abiding in the thing itself, nor merely the capacity to perceive possessed by the perceiving subject, but the power to create both sight and light and light because of sight. We don't see because there is light but, rather, there is light because we see.[54]

13. Between Beings and Things

But something must be there, you insist, something that remains, that persists, that subsists, even when we have ceased to raise it to sensation—and so, gradually you substitute the abstract with the concrete and take *being* to be a *thing*.

---

53   Pedro Antonio Alacrón, *The Scandal*, p. 259.
54   "[F]or light is to be defined only as the sensation produced in the eye of an animal, under given conditions; those same conditions being, to a stone, only warmth or chemical influence, but not light." John Ruskin, *Aratra Pentelici: Six Lectures on the Elements of Sculpture*, Lecture Three, section 99 (p. 84).

It is a common mistake, and a fatal one, for it will become a permanent and insurmountable obstacle that shall block your every attempt to understand either the divine or the human being. It is easy to understand why that is; for if you take being to be static like some-*thing* (instead of *ex*-static like some be-*ing*), then, when you look at man, you will see only a thing, and if you look for God you shall find no-thing, so that, like the fool in the Psalms, you might say in your heart, "There is no God!"

It is not, however, only a mistake, an error in judgement to treat beings as things—it is deception, and the worse kind of deception, for we do so for no other reason than because we find it more *convenient* and more *comfortable* to deal with things than having to deal with beings. This is the accusation that I make against all of us, and I stand by it! And I bring as evidence the fact that, when I asked you which of the two senses you would prefer to lose, if you had to choose, sight or hearing, you all confessed unanimously that you would rather be deprived of beings by becoming deaf than things by becoming blind. It is *things* that we hold dear, it is *things* that we desire, and even when we desire beings, we desire them as *things* and only as long as they are serviceable and instrumental for us *to use*.

For example, notice how our public interactions with people become easier once we reduce others to their functions. At a restaurant, my interaction with my waiter consists precisely in knowing the right words and phrases that function like passwords and passphrases which prompt and activate a certain response. The script of the interaction between waiter and customer, even though it allows for variations, is very specific, and those variations are also scripted. Any break, any interruption of the social pantomime, is considered bad taste and will make everyone involved uncomfortable.

If you were to recognize in these descriptions something automatic and mechanical, you would be right. You remember that one of the things that makes our technology so alluring to us is that it puts us in control and makes out of an unstable world a controlled environment. And a controlled environment is first and foremost *comfortable*, because it removes the anxiety of living in a world of continuous change where other irrational forces are in control instead of us. Art—that is, the artificial—and language (which is in itself artificial) domesticate the world for us: They make it orderly and habitable.

Neither control nor comfort, however, are to be expected when facing the unknown in us and above us; in facing, that is, the human or divine being. To make out of either some-*thing* is to hide oneself (but also to hide *from* oneself one's true Self and the living God), behind a self-made idol.

We see less clearly since our eyes were opened and we see less because we see—constantly—ourselves. Everywhere we turn, we see our reflection. We never see quite clearly. Our vision is impeded by the filters our character, our preferences, our vices, our desires apply to the world around us so that the end result is heavily distorted. Another man standing where I stand, seeing what I see, would describe things very differently from me. He would evaluate things differently. More importantly, even I myself—but a younger or older version of myself— would perceive the same scene differently. I would see things, as we sometimes say, *under a different light.*[55]

Yet, if we are able to go on living, it is thanks to this illusion. It would be unbearable should "the channels of waters appear and the foundations of the world be laid

---

55 [L.L.] All of this punning on my surname cannot have been accidental!

bare" (Ps. 18:16) before our eyes; it would be unbearable, for example, to become cognizant of the movement of our planet, which science confirms but our eyes deny. As it would be equally unbearable to see ourselves, our bodies, as physical objects in a three-dimensional space. We are also spared that reality by a helpful illusion. In our perception of ourselves and of our world we are protected from reality (what the mind claims, and partly creates, as real) by the veil of illusion.

14. Radio Analogy

My grandmother had, in her house where I used to spend many hours during my childhood, a radio. It was a big wooden box, and the front of it, besides the two big knobs and the red needle that moved up and down a line with the various frequencies marked on it, was covered with plaid wicker or rattan from which the sound came. It was clear to me as a child that the interior of the radio was partly hollow and it must have been that space, I concluded, that was inhabited by the little people—they must have been little if they could fit in that small space—who spoke and sung and announced the news through the radio. I was certain that, should I tear the radio open, I would find them there, and as a result of that thought, I was very much tempted to do so.

I see you smiling at the simplicity of that childish thought. Permit me then to smile at your naivete when I hear you talk of your brains as if it contained your thoughts, your memories, your emotions. I don't doubt that the brain is an instrument as precise and impressive as the inner mechanism of a radio, but the voice that speaks through it is not contained in it; it comes, like the voices and sounds transmitted by the radio—*from elsewhere.*

15. Discourse on the Soul

You are aware in yourselves of having a part of you that is visible to you and to others, that we call the body, and a part of you that is invisible to you and to others, although it communicates itself in different ways that are expressed by changes in the body, but the primary mode of communication is speaking through the body (*personare*). It is that invisible part that speaks every time it says "I" to refer to itself as feeling and thinking and making mistakes. Seeing itself as different from the body, it says "I take care of my body because I live in it." For a long time that part of ourselves used to be called the "soul." Today, whatever is left of it, goes by many other names—the mind, consciousness, self, person, identity and so on.

The human soul has three powers:

a)   It animates: This is the primary power of the soul— to which it gives its name: *anima*. The soul is the life of all living things (animals). It is what quickens and wakens in all living things. It is called "vegetation" in trees and plants and "animation" in animals and human beings.

b)   It motivates: That is, it moves. First of all, it moves itself (self-moving, *autokineton*, is the definition found in Plato), and, through the body, it moves the body in space and other bodies in space. It moves when it grows and when it ages, when it is healthy and when it falls ill, it moves in pleasure and in pain. It moves the world, but it is also moved by the world. These interactions, between our soul and our world, *make* sense and sensation. Therefore, it senses. (Sensation is most noticeable in animals, but I don't think it is lacking in plants.) And, finally,

c)   It thinks: That is, it also moves in time and it makes time. It not only senses what it sees—that is, what *is*—but also what is *not*. In fact, it sees this *not*, the not-there, not-here (the absence, the negation, the lack in things): These are the sorceries of imagination. It oscillates between the not-anymore of the past by means of memory and the not-yet of the future by means of expectation. Here, the soul divides itself and is divided.

You can deny that the soul exists, but you cannot deny that the denier exists. The trickery of language can be seen in the case of what we call "the soul," because, as soon as we give it an objective name that somehow makes it a thing, and a thing distinct and separate from us, we see no contradiction in denying it. But if we were rather to refer to the soul by a different name, and better yet by a different expression, periphrastically, so as to avoid making an abstractum into a concretum or mistaking an act for a substance (that constant temptation of the human mind against which William James warns us). Let us translate the noun "the soul" into the expression *that-which-says-I*. It now becomes much more difficult to declare that "*that-which-says-I* does not exist," for it is I who say, "that *that-which-says-I* does not exist" and the saying contradicts the said.

Those who deny the existence of the soul understand that the soul is not an entity and they are right; but their understanding limits existence to entities, to entitative beings, to a some-*thing*. They don't deny, however, (how could they?) the *functions* of the soul, which they ascribe to some other aspect of matter. We are used to somehow thinking of the soul as something, even though we know that at times we are happy and at times we are sad, and those states mean that the soul changes—its *complexion* and its *aspect*, so to speak, change—and so does our thinking, and our being, for at times we are good and at times we are evil and, therefore, it is not a question of a good or evil soul, but of the number of times we allow our soul to change into the one or the other, and for how long it has dwelled in one place or another. It is, therefore, not necessary to suppose that there must be some immutable *thing* lying under the changes through which the soul manifests itself. Perhaps that's why the dessert fathers (of all people!) said that the garment of the body reflects the garment of the soul—that is to say, one thinks and acts as one dresses. Maybe because what we call emotions and thoughts are nothing but the soul's fashion. What logical or metaphysical requirement necessitates that the soul, if it is to exist, must be static?

Now, you are all familiar with the concept of the body needing certain nutrients, like minerals and vitamins, and that the better the body is nourished, the better it does what a body is supposed to do. Similarly, that invisible part of yourselves that we call the soul needs its own kind of nourishment that is, like itself, invisible. The body, that is visible, is fed with visible food, and the soul, that is invisible, is fed with invisible food: That invisible food is the thoughts and ideas we find in a book and the feelings and emotions born in us when we listen to music; it is the satisfaction we feel when we have made something with our hands or restored something broken; and it is also the joy we feel in the company of others. And just as a fare of good quality—with fresh, unprocessed foods—makes the body healthier and stronger, so too does higher quality music and literature nourish our souls and make us healthier in spirit. We are as good as the books we read. (Proof of this is principle is on tragic display in the academy where scholars either read only what other scholars have badly written—so that bad writing has come to be considered good reading—or stop reading altogether.)

I propose that you think of your soul as a seed of spirit within the flesh of that pericarp we call our bodies. Think of that seed naively, as we see sometimes drawn in the margins of old books of botany or alchemy, a homunculus that needs to be fed with its own kind of food as often as you feed the body, and remember that you have to give it not only what is essential for its nourishment, but also little things to amuse and please it. These your homunculus derives from a process very similar to bodily digestion called *reading*. And please don't forget that your homunculus has a spiritual mouth and a spiritual stomach—the stomach of the mind, as St. Augustine calls memory—and spiritual eyes too, which, once opened, are capable of seeing what the eyes of the body cannot see.

The Impromptu

Sermon Over the Boar's Head

(Given at the Faculty Club)

After three long lectures, it was finally time for dinner. Upon entering the great Dining Hall, I noticed a blackboard on my left side which read: "Today's Menu." And under that, scrawled in white chalk in timid calligraphy, were the following options:

Salad of flowering tarragon,
Hummingbirds *en brochette*,
Zucchini stuffed with puppy brains,
Plover roasted in vine leaves,
Sautéed ram's cheek,
Ewe's tails.

I had the impression that no poem, no epic among the ancient bards, rhapsodized more unspeakable cruelties than the six verses that made up this carnivorous epitaph. Wishing, however, not to offend my hosts, I kept my silence, hoping to distract myself with any other sound or sight that might come my way, anything to distract me from the noise of smacking lips devouring dead meat. At one of the tables, the one nearest to the raised platform where they sat me along with the President and some of the faculty that were in attendance at my lectures, a heated debate was boiling up. I couldn't make out what it was about, except for a few stray expressions that caught my ear, which seemed to indicate that they were arguing over whether croissants were preferable to Swiss cheese. It was only much later that I realized they were not talking about accoutrement, but two essays published in some obscure student periodical.[56]

Speaking of cheese, I remember that the cheese that day, placed elegantly on an acacia board and served with a set of

---

56 [L.L.] Not without considerable difficulty have I managed to identify these two essays as "I Love Croissants, or Why No Mosque Should be Built Near Ground Zero" and "On Swiss Cheese" published in *The Fenwick Review* on September 2010 and November 2024 respectively.

tortoiseshell knives, was half a wheel of Baron Bigod from Senex.

"The real question, my good fellas," *said President Joseph while spreading a thick layer of the cheese on his bread,* "is 'who was this Baron Bigod?' What sort of man would have himself associated with such flavorful cheese?"

"Was he soft and spreadable?" *added Burnop the turnip scornfully.*

"And yeasty!" *shouted Fr. Beauchard with a shudder of disdain.*

"That explains those cheesy fingermarks on the margins of the Magna Carta," *said another.*

He—Beauchard that is—ate his food from the plate in front of him with his thumb and index finger, which he then kept pressed together for the remainder of the meal, as priests used to do with their liturgical digits after holding the host, lest any particle of the consecrated bread fall to the ground. This forced him to hold the handle of his teacup only with his ring finger and his pinky, and in that precarious fashion, he brought it to his lips to take a sip. Of course, I knew that Beauchard was a priest, but I was already suspecting that he had some skeletons hidden in the armoire.[57] I remember that he was making the following argument:

"If you have to ask someone for a favor—a woman to marry you, or to divorce you; an unmerited promotion from your superiors," (*when he said this, I noticed that he was looking directly at Burnop*), "do it over a meal. To eat, to be reminded that you are flesh, like the flesh you eat, is to bring you down from the lofty heights of the I, of him who says 'I' when he says 'I do this' and 'I am that,' to the body that you are and its digestive system. After a meal we are

---

57 [L.L.] A suspicion that J.P. Madrox seems to confirm (see, *The Philosopher King*, Eugene, Oregon: Cascade Books, 2024).

more human because we have been more animal—not because we are capable of thinking, but because we have done what any animal must do: Eat. Then the request, coming from an animal to a fellow animal with whom one has just shared a meal, finds its recipient less guarded behind our imperious 'I' and more open to the world, part of which has just been ingested with every bite. All I am saying," *he concluded*, "is if you want something done (or forgiven), you must be willing to break bread."

My attention was suddenly interrupted by the magnificent entrance of the roasted boar's head on a silver plate carried by two Fenwickians. The boar's head is, of course, Fenwick's signature dish and is prepared and brought out ceremoniously whenever a celebration is afoot.

"Only Lamb knows how to roast a pig," *quipped the President who was of course referring to the great essayist Charles Lamb and, in particular his* "Dissertation upon Roast Pig."

"They don't write dissertations like that anymore," *Beauchard remarked.*

"And some can't write dissertations at all," *said the President raising his eyebrow in the direction of Burnop, who, as he was seated on the same side of the table, failed to notice.*

When the platter carrying the roasted head of the poor beast was placed—in my honor, I suppose—before me, I spent a few minutes contemplating the offering I couldn't accept and, after a brief time, I stood up from my chair, and with a passionate voice filled with indignation, addressed my fellow symposiasts thusly:

My dear Colleagues and all of you—Young Fenwickians,

As one should kill only what one is prepared to eat, so you should not eat what you haven't killed! No man should be allowed to eat what he himself hasn't killed with his own hands. I can't expect that any of you possess the skill and strength required to hunt your dinner down but at least be man enough to have the courage to look your victim in the eye before you take, out of him, a bite. As it is, you are the most cowardly of carnivorous animals: Scavengers! You expect others to do your killing and butchering and packaging and—*my God!*—even cooking and delivering for you. You buy your fruits already peeled, your salads already washed, your vegetables cut, your olives pitted, your juices squeezed! You have just enough strength to raise your feeble hands to your mouth with a fork, you good-for-nothing scoundrels! If your stomach desires meat, then you should stomach the gore and brutality that comes with obtaining it.

Woe to you, hypocrites! If you want to eat the flesh of another animal, don't do it here, with your linen tablecloths and your porcelain plates and the background music to expunge your crimes. Do it in the slaughterhouse, with the stench of steaming blood and gore rising from the ground and the bellows of your dinner in your ears begging for its life!

Woe to you, hypocrites! You don't say pig but pork, you call it beef, not the cow it was. And now, worse than any other insult, *protein*. The carte-blanche of your cowardice. You hide behind words. That animal gave its life to become your dinner, at least save its dignity and call it by its name.

Woe to you, hypocrites! What kind of life do you think you have if it is sustained by the death of others? You are all death-eaters. Everything you eat must first die so that you may live. Look at our modern, efficient, and sterile kitchens: Don't they look like morgues and mortuaries? The same stainless-steel appliances, the same protocols of cleanness, the same principles of hygiene.

Woe to your, hypocrites! Your bellies have become the graves of so many animal corpses that you stink of death every time you open your mouths! These are not stomachs, these are *sarcophagi* of flesh and flesh-eating flesh!

You are not satisfied with stealing their milk and their eggs, you require their skin as well, for it is true what has been said: "A jarred palate requires a pickle." A jarred palate is, of course, only the last sign of a man enfeebled by his passions, by going always one step further, by asking always a little bit more. So that he now needs the jolt of a pickle's vinegar in order to feel.

I would like before I close my eyes for the last time to think of all those animals who died so I can live. Those who were flayed and skinned, killed and dismembered, not so that I can live—for nothing that came from their deaths was essential for my living—but so that I can live *comfortably*—with a comfort that sickened me unto death. I would like to think of them so that I can be reminded that it is only fair and just that I too should follow them and die as they did.

Whereupon, to my astonishment, a general uproar of my audience occurred, consisting of a loud cacophony of shouts, accompanied by many violent gesticulations. I have never, anywhere seen the likes of it, before or since![58] *Some angry students were banging their dinner trays on their tables (thankfully, I thought, our administration at Holy Cross had banished all trays from Kimball Hall back in 2009 by using some ridiculous "environmental" excuse). And there was I, the center of this rage. The possibility of continuing with our dinner was not even mooted and I consider myself most fortunate to have escaped unharmed.*

---

58   Except, of course, in the notorious case Prof. Leo C. Ferrari as he relates, in almost the same words, in his commentary on Book Eight of the *Confessions* in Kim Paffenroth and Robert P. Kennedy (eds.), *A Reader's Companion to Augustine's Confessions,* (Louisville, Westminster John Knox Press, 2003, p. 136).

My eloquent outburst seemed to have caused a great offense to Fenwick University's pride, their tradition, and even their identity. The boar's head was more important to them than I had thought.[59] *Amidst the general uproar President Joseph rose to his feet—not without some effort and a great deal more displeasure—and gave me a curt dismissal with the words:* "We shall hear from you again, sir!" *I was then escorted out of the Faculty Club and sent back to my lodgings where I soon realized that it would be very difficult for me to continue with my lectures after that evening's affair without some form of reconciliation or at least an apology.*

Thus, I sent later that night a note to President Joseph explaining, among other things, that while fasting saves and preserve, feasting spends and destroys and that there is no celebration without sacrifice. That a loss—loss of goods or loss of life—is required for every feast. Therefore, the question of eating meat, I said, ought to be examined as part of this economy of life and death. Then I asked to which gods it is that we sacrifice our daily consumption of meat and what is it that we celebrate so frantically? Are we capable of feasting when we have forgotten how to fast? Isn't this perhaps the condition of our malaise manifested through so many pathological symptoms that affect ever increasingly both the person and the polis—namely, that, contrary to all appearances, we have become incapable of celebration? I concluded my note with a most abject apology, and I asked for the favor of being allowed to apologize publicly—since it was my public comments that had caused scandal and offense to the Fenwick community—by offering some appropriate thoughts I had prepared on the subject of sin and repentance. Let that be my public confession—if only he, in his Presidential magnanim-

---

59   To cite only one, the most obvious, example: Fenwick University's official motto, "Quot estis in convivio," comes from the "Boar's Head Carol." Naturally, Fenwick students prefer an apocryphal version of the motto, "Quot testis in convivio."

ity, would be willing to afford me the occasion of addressing his community one last time.

The President's response came the next morning.

The Night Vigil of the Third Day

Apologia Pro Vita Sua

*O*n *the morning of the third day, the same messenger as the day before was sent to my rooms, this time with the President's response to my note. President Joseph was returning the accusation that I had thrown at him and his Fenwick colleagues the evening before, calling me a hypocrite, only he did so in a manner infinitely more tactful than I had done. His response was a few written lines that I immediately recognized as taken from St. Isaac the Syrian's* Ascetical Homilies: "And when you fill your stomach, do not shamelessly search out matters and concepts concerning God, lest you later repent of it. Understand what I say: there can be no knowledge of the mysteries of God on a full stomach."

"Is he calling me fat?" *I asked.*

Louis Light smiled at me without saying a word, as if the answer were too obvious to affirm.

"St. Thomas Aquinas," *I said while handing him back the President's response,* "would beg to differ with your President on that point."

"He *did* accept your request," *Light said,* "although on one condition."

"What's that?" *I asked suspiciously.*

"That you give your last lecture during the night. The memory of last night's episode is still fresh. We suggest that you dine alone in your room tonight and meet us afterwards, but not at the lecture hall. After what happened last night, we expect fewer people in attendance, so we have moved your lecture to the seminar room."

When I took my seat at the oak table in the large seminar room that evening, it was already after ten o'clock.

I will now speak to you about sin, *I said.*

On what authority? you ask.

But, of course, that of a sinner. Here at last is a subject of which we are all experts. Let us not be like those fools, those "single individuals" who are stupid enough to pose the question "What is sin?" as if we didn't already have a pretty good idea. You remember Kierkegaard's admonition: "When the single individual is stupid enough to inquire about sin as if it were something foreign to him, he only asks as a fool."

1. Of Sin and Sinners

First of all, four clarifications are in order:

The first point of clarification regarding sin is that *it is the sinner that makes the sin*—and not the other way around. One does not become a sinner by sinning (Aristotle). Rather one sins because one is (*born*) a sinner (Augustine). This competition, Aristotle versus Augustine, will take place under a pear tree. And it is Augustine that comes out victorious. But of that later. Here you have this little idea with tremendous implications that has become the most despised of all Christian doctrines: *the doctrine of the original sin*. Before you cast your stone, please answer these two questions:

a) When you want to excuse yourself of your sin don't you say, "It is human nature after all" or "It is only natural"? By talking in this fashion, are you not taking sin to be coterminous with human nature?

b) If we are not born sinners, then we must have been born innocent. But none of us here could make the claim of being innocent now. Therefore, the burden is on you to tell us *when* exactly and how you lost your baby-like innocence.

The doctrine of the original sin makes another interesting, and equally anomalous, point: That, when it comes to sin, we are all experts is, in itself, both perplexing and problematic. After all, we don't find such universal expertise with regards to any other subject. It is only sin that is democratic; the Good, on the other hand, is *hierarchic*: that is, orderly, and beautiful. (I allude here to the theory of universals: the *bonum* is also the *pulchrum*; *bonum* because *pulchrum*; and never *bonum* unless also *pulchrum*.)

The second clarification with regards to sin is that what makes something a sin is not a *thing* (here one discerns the first temptation coming from and in the form of the Gnostic dualism) but our *disposition* towards things. The object of sin is always something in itself good (it cannot be anything else for if it is created, it was created by God, and is thus good). What makes something sinful is *how* one desires it. That's why it is impossible to produce a list of sins (although we do so for practical or pastoral reasons), but even in the canonical list of seven (or more) deadly (or not) sins, what is named is, if you pay attention, not a thing, not some-*thing*, but a *disposition* towards things. Gluttony, for example—my favorite sin for obvious reasons—does not blame the food but its abuse. Envy does not blame the other's goods but one's inability to be happy that another has such goods, and so on.

Vices can become virtues and *vice versa*. For example, philanthropy, almsgiving, and charity are generally regarded as good and noble things, but when one gives to the poor assuming for oneself the role of savior, thinking, perhaps, that one is better than those one helps, doesn't such an attitude make one's donation sinful? On the other hand, lying is a very bad thing—even if we have forgotten this truth as we now live in a world of lies and liars—so much so that Christ calls the devil not "the father of adultery and fornication," not "the father of murders," but "the father of lies" (John 8:44). Yet I know of a man who became a saint because he lied to the police who came to his monastery looking for a criminal. The criminal had indeed visited the monastery and had confessed, unbeknownst to him, to killing the saint's brother. Still, the future saint offered him a means of escape and lied to the police who came looking for him. Our list of sins, then, suggests an orientation of the mind and the heart towards a particular object or action without necessarily designating those things as sinful in themselves.

It is the disposition of the heart that makes a sin a sin. In particular, the selfish disposition, for as we think of the various kinds of sin and what each has in common with the others, we quickly realize that each is self-centered. Sins seek self-affirmation, self-gratification, self-promotion, self-satisfaction, and so on. In short, they are all *selfish*. Even though sin comes in every variety to suit every taste, each shares the same root: *the self*.

The third point of clarification is that we must remember that arguments and logic—that is, reason—are rarely, if ever, successful in combating sin (otherwise it would have been enough for Augustine to stop at the intellectual conversion of Book VII of the *Confessions*); when it comes to sin and evil, one finds oneself pitted against an *impression*, not a *position* to be debated, but a *deception* to be exposed.

And finally, the fourth point of clarification is what follows from the above, namely that sin is idiotic (See, *Confessions* XII. 25. 34). This is a point that St. Augustine explains better elsewhere, in his long treatise *On the Holy Trinity* (*De Trinitate*), book XII, 3. 14 which I quote:

> What happens is that the soul, loving its own power [see Nietzsche's "Will to Power"] slides away from the whole which is common to all into the part which is its own private property. By following God's directions and being perfectly governed by his laws it could enjoy the whole universe of

creation; but by the apostasy of pride which is called the beginning of sin it strives to grab something more than the whole and to govern it by its own laws [auto-nomy]; and because there is nothing more than the whole it is thrust back into anxiety over a part, and so by being greedy for more it gets less. That is why greed is called the root of all evils. Thus all that it tries to do on its own [auto-archy] against the laws that govern the universe it does by its own body, which is the only part it has a part-ownership in [cf., "my body, my rights"]. And so it finds delight in bodily shapes and movements, and because it has not got them with it inside, it wraps itself in their images which it has fixed in the memory. In this way it defiles itself foully with a fanciful sort of fornication by referring all its business to one or other of the following ends: curiosity [*concupiscentia oculorum*/lust of the eyes], searching for bodily and temporal experience through the senses; swollen conceit, affecting to be above other souls which are given over to their senses [*superbia vitae*/arrogance, lust for glory and fame]; or carnal pleasure [*conscupiscentia carnis*/lust of the flesh], plunging itself in this muddy whirlpool.

In this passage, Augustine—speaking of (lying) language as originating in the original sin—seems to suggest that private property, the very notion of ownership, is—in the words of Fr. Hill in one of his notes on this paragraph—"a kind of mark of Cain, the stigma of man alienated from God." At the end of this paragraph, Augustine returns to the tripartite structure of the sinful configuration (*Gestell*) of the world—that is, to the triple affirmation of what is my own:

a) My own pleasure (*conscupiscentia carnis*),
b) My own power (*concupiscentia oculorum*),
c) My own name (*superbia*).

In order to understand what is implied here, ask yourself this question: What is the relation between these two monastic vows, the vow of abstinence and the vow of poverty? Fr. Beauchard has claimed that "one cannot keep one of the vows without also keeping the other." He must know something.

Can you imagine what would happen to all industries and institutions across governments and markets if everyone were to become a monk, living in voluntary poverty and in voluntary sexual abstinence? The world would collapse. But that's precisely the point. Here you have the connection. The world would collapse because the world is built upon ownership:

> Make sure you understand this, beloved. It is on account of what we own individually that litigation is instituted and enmity, quarrels, and fights break out. Uproar, dissensions, scandals, sins, unjust actions, and even homicide are all the result of private ownership. What are we fighting over? Over the thing we call our own. We do not go to law about things we possess in common, do we?[60]

Civilization was built by possession (Cain). And possession is fratricidal. For if I have something, that means you don't have it. "No one puts bread into his belly without depriving the belly of another."[61]

But to "appropriate" in this sense is also to "divide"— its ideal of independence is at the same time an ideal of isolation, the isolation of economic and moral self-sufficiency. Furthermore, the greed for property for temporal goods is inevitably exclusive and monopolistic. "For he who desires the glory of possession would feel that his power was diminished, if he were obliged to share it with any living associate." Secular society may thus discover

---

60 Augustine, *Expositions of the Psalms*, translated by Maria Boulding, O.S.B., Exposition of Psalm 131, (New York: New City Press, 2004, vol, III/20, p. 159).
61 Matthew Clemente, *Bacchus Agonistes*, (Boston: Senex Press, 2024), p. 3 (Cf. fn13, fn28, & fn32 above.)

its prototype in Babylon, "the city of confusion," hopelessly rent by schism and dissension it cannot overcome. And since "Cain signifies possession," it may look to the fratricide as its founder and first citizen.[62]

Every citizen then is citizen Cain.

2. Sciences of Sin

In addition to these four points of clarification, I need to call your attention to what I call the three sciences of sin, namely the fact that sin is a phenomenon that corrodes three abilities in particular of the human being:

a) His ability to know (epistemology),
b) His ability to govern himself (economy), and
c) His ability to be himself, that is, to be good and just (ethics).

Sin as an epistemological category: Sin implies and affects a distortion in how one perceives things. *What gravity is for the body desire is for the mind.* That is axiomatic. And all sin feeds on desire, whatever that desire might be: for pleasure, for power, for glory. Our particular vices arrange and color the world differently, and the same world, even the same word, would acquire a different sense and interpretation to others with other vices and other desires. Sin is a filter (a hermeneutical filter), and therefore it affects how we see, that is, how we know the world and ourselves. As sin becomes often a lifestyle (or the basis around which one builds one's life), so too can it become a world-view, an ideology. It should not come as a surprise that he who has one of these two often has the other as well. That is to say, we often believe what-

---

62 Cochrane, *Christianity and Classical Culture*, pp. 542-543.

ever rationalizes our choices and construct worldviews to justify our vice.

Old sins cast long shadows, they say. And original sin is the oldest. I often see in the other person the shadow of my sin, and I see the world around me darkened by that same shadow. It is because of this, I believe, that the most accurate picture we can garner of ourselves comes by observing what angers us and what we find offensive in others and recognizing that as our shadow. One must remember, however, that shadows are distortive images— false images of ourselves.

I can sense that you don't like Augustine and want a more modern witness. Very well. Take the witness of phenomenology then. Husserl has described a particular attribute of consciousness, namely its narrowness, that explains why our *attention* can only be directed at one thing at a time. Sin is the state of a consciousness that has become disorderly self-referential (*oculus curvus in se*, to paraphrase Luther's Latin). It can only see itself or it sees itself cast onto everything that it sees ("and their eyes were opened and they saw themselves" Gen 3:7—I spoke at some length and rather beautifully, if I do say so, of that verse yesterday as you will, no doubt, remember). Which means that this opening of the eyes, insofar as one's eyes open to one's self, becomes blind to everything else. Sin, therefore, is an epistemological category that must be taken into account when we build world-theories and theories of knowledge. "For evils, of which there is no number, surrounded me; My transgressions of the law laid hold of me, *and I was not able to see*" (Ps. 39:12).

Sin as an economical category: You can tell as much, if not more, about the character of a man by looking at his bank account as you can surmise by reading his personal diary. And sin spends. Save your soul and you also save your money. See also the fourth point of clarification above on the idiocy of sin.

Sin as ethical category: *Hamartia* is often translated as "missing the mark," but "failing to catch" might be more appropriate. Our sin is always the sin of failing to respond to the invitation that God addresses to us through each moment (of *kairos*). If you could see with spiritual eyes, you would see a vast number of those unanswered moments loitering around you: Those are all the moments that some-One was throwing a ball to you, hoping you would catch it and throw it back—that's all you had to do—but you didn't it, most likely because you were distracted looking at your own reflection. It is out of this vast number of missed opportunities that we forge the chain of regrets we wear, as Jacob Marley wore his. And these chains make us heavy—the heaviness that is witnessed by our lack of levity. That saints have been said to levitate should not surprise us. What else do you expect to be the result of one making oneself so *light*?[63]

3. Sin's Wages

Sin has effects. And so, he who knew what was right and chose *not* to do it will lose that which he refused to use. His *knowledge* will become dim and diminished. And he who willed *not* to do what is good, while he was able to do it, will lose what he refused to use. His *will* will weaken, and he will become unable to do what is good even if he wants to.

> It is the most just penalty of sin that man should lose what he was unwilling to make a good use of, when he could have done so without difficulty if he had wished. It is just that he who, knowing what is right, does not do it should lose the

---

63   [L.L.] ☺

capacity to know what is right, and he who had the power to do what is right and would not should lose the power to do it when he is willing. In fact there are for every sinful soul these two penal conditions, ignorance and difficulty. From ignorance springs disgraceful error, and from difficulty comes painful effort.[64]

If you demand proof of this double disability, listen to the confessions of this eloquent drunkard:

> Twelve years ago I was possessed of a healthy frame of mind and body. I was never strong, but I think my constitution (for a weak one) was as happily exempt from the tendency to any malady as it was possible to be. I scarce knew what it was to ail anything. Now, except when I am losing myself in a sea of drink, I am never free from those uneasy sensations in head and stomach, which are so much worse to bear than any definite pains or aches.

> At that time I was seldom in bed after six in the morning, summer and winter.[65] I awoke refreshed, and seldom without some merry thoughts in my head, or some piece of a song to welcome the new-born day. Now, the first feeling which besets me after stretching out the hours of recumbence to their last possible extent, is a forecast of the wearisome day that lies before me, with a secret wish that I could have lain on still, or never awaked.

There is a *tunc* and *nunc* here as well, as in the *Confessions*, except, notice well, it has been reversed: "then I was mis-

---

64   Augustine, *De Libero Arbitrio*, III. 18.52, p. 202.
65   Compare this to the famous first line of Proust's masterpiece: "For a long time I would go to bed early," which immediately signals a deterioration in the character of the narrator. If he used to go to bed early (or *happy*, if one were to take *bonne heure* as *bonheur*), that means he doesn't anymore. Something happened that brought this change in his habits, an evil influence is suggested, a dark habit, for whatever accounts for that change has now become fixed. "For a long time I would go to bed early" can be taken to mean "A long time ago I was happy."

erable, now I am happy" says Augustine, and that's why his *Confessions* are a long prayer of thanksgiving that leads to that opening, "Great are you, oh Lord...!" "Then I was happy, now I am miserable," says Charles Lamb and his "Confessions" are the confession of a weakness and a weakened self:

> Business which though never very particularly adapted to my nature, yet as something of necessity to be gone through, and therefore best undertaken with cheerfulness, I used to enter upon with some degree of alacrity, now wearies, affrights, perplexes me. I fancy all sorts of discouragements, and am ready to give up an occupation which gives me bread, from a harassing conceit of incapacity. The slightest commission given me by a friend, or any small duty which I have to perform for myself, as giving orders to a tradesman, etc., haunts me as a labor impossible to be got through. So much the springs of action are broken.

> The same cowardice attends me in all my intercourse with mankind. I dare not promise that a friend's honor, or his cause, would be safe in my keeping, if I were put to the expense of any manly resolution in defending it. So much the springs of moral action are deadened within me.[66]

At the end of this essay, a law is discovered operating of which Augustine had already warned us: Reason and will, when impaired by addiction, are not able to operate unless under the influence of the vice for the sake of which they lost their vitality in the first place:

> *[R]eason shall only visit him through intoxication*; for it is a fearful truth, that the intellectual faculties by repeating acts of intemperance may be driven from their orderly sphere of action, their clear daylight ministries, until they shall be brought at last to depend, for the faint manifesta-

---

66 Charles Lamb, *A Complete Elia*, (New York: The Heritage Press, 1943), pp. 355-6.

tion of their departing energies, upon the returning periods of the fatal madness to which they owe their devastation. The drinking man is never less himself than during his sober intervals.[67]

Because he is now the *drinking* man, the *drinking* man he is does not feel himself unless he is drinking, and the sinning man does not feel himself except in his sin. To the sinner qua sinner, sin is of course normal and rational— he has already rationalized his choice and justified his action.

4. A Presidential Interruption

"Excuse me!" *said President Joseph rising to his feet.* "Excuse me for interrupting you. But since we are here in this seminar room listening to more of you at this late hour, after our dinners and, if I can speak of myself, after a few drinks," *he said raising the glass he held in his hand,* "perhaps I am allowed to make a comment?" *He formed that sentence as a question, but he meant it as a rhetorical one, for before I had a chance to give a response, he continued:* "I think that we haven't given proper attention to the euphoria that the various forms of intoxication (that's one way of putting it; "inspiration" might be a better word) provide us. Is this kind of inspiration to be dragged through the mud while the other, the 'good' inspiration of poets and prophets, is praised and exulted only because this one," *he said referring to his glass,* "is artificial? Baudelaire wrote of *les Paradis artificiels*—are they any less Paradisiac because not natural? Don't we extract almost all of them from nature? Or is it because this is an inspiration on command, as an inspiration, I concede, ought not to be (if it is from the Spirit who blows when

---

67   Charles Lamb, *A Complete Elia*, p. 355.

and where He wills)? Yet wouldn't you agree that it makes you not only happy but also *better*? At least it makes you *feel* better."

"It mimics the gestures of joy," *I said.*

"Are you, then, dismissing the power that imitation has in realizing its goals?" *he asked.*

"What do you mean?" *I said, not sure to which ancient or modern discussion of mimesis he might be referring.*

"Every night," *he said,* "don't we all fall asleep by *faking* being asleep?"

"A good example," *I said with satisfaction,* "that's exactly what your 'inspiration' is: A lulling of the mind and the senses—putting your *self* to sleep. It is, furthermore," *I continued,* "an offence against the goodness of the reality and of the life from which you seek to escape."

"Life may be good," *he interjected sardonically in order to add after a moment's pause,* "but we are *not.* Not always, at least." *He added as if a dark memory has passed through his mind.* "And a good man has every reason (I won't say 'right') to want to take leave from his bad self."

"Perhaps," *I responded.* "But at the end of the day you accrued a debt that sooner or later you are called to pay."

"How do you mean?" *the President said, a little annoyed that his previous remark was not the final word of our exchange as he had thought (or wished) it to be.*

"The artificial pleasure is like credit in the economy of pleasure," *I said.* "There are only so many genuine moments of joy that are permitted to any of us mortals. Thus the little artificial joys one procures during the day (sometimes even before lunch) are pleasures withdrawn prematurely and, as I said, quite literally, doing that accrues a debt that sooner or later one is called to pay either by his deteriorating health or—"*and here I pause to look at him,* "by his diminished sensibility."

(Throughout the following, President Joseph's posture and facial expression underwent a gradual change brought about by recognizing his of affliction in my discussion of addiction. At times, he turned red and then pale, at other times I could see his eyes welling up with tears, or him trying to hide his trembling hands. These changes, however, were indicative of a change that he was undergoing mysteriously in the depths of his heart—and I surmise that it amounted to nothing less than the resolution to change his ways.)

5. Illusory Freedom

Freedom is never freedom to do something but rather freedom from compulsion: I am free by not having to do something. It is in the very character of freedom to liberate but freedom-to, as in the freedom-to-do-something, is only a disguised *attachment*. When we demand our freedom, to the point that we are ready to die for it, and when we value independence as our highest good, we do so in the name of a false freedom. We want to be free, but not *from* sin (that freedom we dread and we flee it), we want to be free *in order to* sin. "I want to be free to do as I please" means "I am bound to as many masters as the objects and the objectives of my will." And here please mark well the following: To get rid of One master does not mean that you are now under none, and thus independent. *The opposite of One is not none, but the Many.* In search of one's independence you exchange the one true Master for a multitude of them. The problem is that you are, in fact, entirely free to do what you want, but you are not free from *what* you want or from wanting (which is not what *you* want, anyways, for desire is mimetic: It imitates the other's desire so as to always want for ourselves that which we think others want for themselves—

but let's leave that for another time). This servitude is
what we understand as freedom, to do as one wills. My
will be done. The ability, the potency to sin, that's what
we understand as our power. *I sin because I can. Posse peccare* (II. 6. 14). But can I not? That I cannot. I cannot free
myself from the freedom to sin. I cannot not sin. *Non posse
non peccare. Non posse*: impotence. "Master, serve!"

When we say, as St. Augustine did a little later on in
his life, "O Lord, give me chastity, but not yet," then we
are at an early stage in spiritual understanding, when we
find ourselves confronted by that dead-end of knowing
that a change is necessary but, no matter how much or
how sincerely we try to change (and I believe that there
are people who have sincerely tried to change) we don't
have the strength to change ourselves. And this is what is
wrong with this attitude: *It understands the whole matter in
terms of strength* (and thus of one's own accomplishment—
but let's leave that aside for the moment).

6. Conversion

They will tell you: "Holiness is difficult." No. It is very
easy. All it takes is doing nothing—that is, doing nothing *more* than that which is required of you, desiring
nothing *more* than what has be allotted to you, giving
up Macbeth's "more-having sauce that makes us hunger
more" (Act IV, Scene 3).

They will tell you: "Holiness is grim and sad." Nothing
could be farther from the truth. Holiness is happiness
and a surprising joy. The saint has for free that for which
the rest of us have paid dearly—not with a pound of our
flesh, but with our whole body and soul—and still would
fail to enjoy. Sin, on the other hand, is always expensive—
and scrutinize this whichever way you like, you will find

it to be true in every sense—even when it seems free: If it doesn't cost money, it costs time, and it always wastes your life and burdens your soul with its ever-increasing debt.

You should never try to change by exchanging pleasure with the lack of pleasure—that is, giving up something for nothing. That will never work. The point is *not* to deprive oneself of one pleasure after another until one is left joyless. Such an attempt is doomed to fail because, in the first place, we are meant to be attracted to pleasure and, secondly, the things that we find pleasurable are so genuinely. (There is no point denying that sin is pleasurable, but thankfully for some people it is not pleasurable *enough*. They are looking for something better.) Change—*transformation* might be a more deserving name, *conversion* is the technical term—can be accomplished only by exchanging pleasure with pleasure (it has to be the same currency), lower pleasure with higher pleasure—which, incidentally, is not any less pleasurable because it is higher, it is higher precisely because it is more pleasurable. If it wasn't (and to the extent that for some people it isn't—*yet*) it wouldn't be able to replace the lower one.

"Then why can we not do it?!" *asked someone from the far end of the table whose face I couldn't see, as other students were blocking him, but whom I recognized from his voice to be Burnop.*

Because the lower pleasure to which you are currently attracted has not yet appeared to you as *lower, I responded*. You don't have yet the *taste* (*sapientia* from which we derive the epithet *sapiens*, as in *homo sapiens*, comes from *sapere*: to taste) that will help you realize that what you now find pleasurable is cheap and low, suitable only for pigs and a poor substitute of a higher pleasure. Most importantly, you don't believe that such a higher pleasure really exists, since, all the people you

know only know of and practice lower pleasures. Here is
the ingenuity of God, however: The lower pleasures precisely because they take as their objects finite and transient things are themselves finite and transient, limited
and fleeting, and therefore, *designed to disappoint*. That's
why sins are repetitive like addictions: One has always
to *return* in order to *retrieve* the initial pleasure that was
subsequently lost. So, one gets trapped in a self-destructive habit.

7. The Example of the Flies

We then behave like flies that get trapped in a room
buzzing around and although a window has been opened
to help them fly out towards the source of light, they
instead keep flying in the opposite direction, towards the
wall where the light reflects. The lower pleasures, which
one is afraid of losing when one asks to be rid of them,
"but not yet," are pleasurable because they are reflec-
tions of the true pleasure. But they will never be able,
no matter how often you return to them, to lead you outside your confinement, into the open air where the true
light and true life come from. (Compare it, if you wish,
to Plato's cave allegory.) The very fact that we need to
return—that is, to repeat the sinful habit—proves that it
has failed to give us what we asked for, namely, happiness. Happy it made us but only briefly. No sooner did we
have it than we have already lost it. That's why I said that
the lower pleasures, precisely because they take as their
objects finite and transient things, are themselves finite
and transient and therefore *designed to disappoint* us.
And disappoint they do. The fleeting happiness, precisely
because it is fleeting, becomes a flashing moment in an
otherwise dark night of frustration and unhappiness, in

a life spent between fear and anxiety. Real objects cast shadows and so do real pleasures. A pleasure's shadow—a sham pleasure as one finds upon pursuing it—is what we have called here a lower pleasure.

8. Exchanges

At this point there are only two possibilities: Either we remain trapped in this vicious cycle of unhappiness or we learn how to exchange the lower pleasure that we now seek with a higher one that we will enjoy more.

"It is not possible!" *that same, grating voice said with an air of resignation.*

But let us look at our own lives, *I said.* How often and how easily have you changed your habits by going, for example, from eating cheap food, to enjoying a meal at a good restaurant? When one has been exposed to a finer cuisine, does he miss not eating the poor-quality fare that he was used to, does he feel deprived of it? How many times in your young lives have you not already said: "I can't believe I used to like that." Another example: A woman falls in love with a man; she begins to date him but soon realizes that her sweetheart is not a person worthy of her love. (*I could see that I had the attention of Dr. Damaris Tighe who was tilting her head so that she didn't miss a word of what was said*). So she ends the relationship. Sometime later, the same woman falls in love with another man who is really worthy of her devotion and trust. Does she regret having broken off her relation with her former lover? Don't you think she would eventually forget about him entirely and, if she recalls him at all, it would be a recollection deprived of all emotion?

That is how a saint recalls his sins and that's how a saint becomes a saint: By exchanging a lower pleasure for a higher, greater, better pleasure. And, finally and most importantly, that's how man can attain happiness.

9. What God Does *Not* Know

Sin, we said, has two effects that lock us into the vicious circle of sinning: *knowledge* becomes partial and distorted, and action becomes *difficult* and onerous. But there is a third that is far more serious and it explains the two others. Sin infects us with a dose of nothingness that corrodes our being. To explain this statement, you must first answer the question "how does God know?" It has been said that God knows everything but how does He come about such an all-encompassing knowledge? He has no eyes, of course, nor any other physical organ by which He is capable of knowing, but if what theologians say about God's simplicity, namely that God's essence is existence, then He is not capable even of the distinction between knower and the thing known, the distinction between the subject and object of knowledge, as we find it in our minds. He knows precisely by this simplicity that knows all things by knowing Himself by whom and through whom and according to whom all things were created. He knows us, to the extent that we conform and abide by the natural patterns by which we were created and insofar as we walk on the paths to which He has called us—but sin is not any of that. If God knows His creation by knowing Himself in whom all the reasons of the Creation (*rationes seminales*) subsist, then God *cannot* know sin. And, therefore, when we sin, we become momentarily invisible to Him, so to speak. It is, however, by means of that knowledge—that is, insofar as God knows us—that we exist. Every sinful act and desire infects us with a dose of nothingness that corrodes and diminishes our being and its capacities. Here we return to the beginning: This weakening becomes manifest in our weakness to know and to act.

10. *Theologia Naturalis*

"What about this God, then?" *said one voice.*

When we speak of "Our Father *who art in heaven*" we don't speak of the celestial old Man known by his depictions from our childhood cartoons with a long white beard seated on some clouds. This visualization (for it is not exactly a conceptualization) has led to the mistake in imagining God as something outside us and far away from us: "In heaven." In the language of the Scriptures, however, "heaven" means simply something like the "blue" in the expression "out of the blue"—that is, the realm of the invisible and the unexpected. God is better imagined as something as intimate to us as our own life and understanding.

God is what in the language of physics is called a Force or Power (Δύναμις); and in the language of metaphysics is recognized as a Principle (Ἀρχή); and in the language of logic, a Law (Λόγος); but a Principle, and a Law, and a Force that is not only *personal*, that is, essentially relational and absolutely free, but also a *Person*.

The difficulty here lies in that we are accustomed to thinking of a Person as something concrete and of forces, principles, and causes as something abstract. For example, that Life and Wisdom are not only *personal*, but a Person—or, rather, that they are personal because they are a Person—is for us a contradiction in terms, "a concrete abstraction."

And a Person that is *not* a being! Here again the difficulty is to think of someone who is this "is." Furthermore, this *Not-Being* becomes, at a particular space and time, in history, a particular, historical *human* being, Jesus Christ (hence, the scandal of incarnation). In the Gospel of St. John, this particular human person, called Jesus (his name means "salvation" in Hebrew) makes a series of extraordinary pronouncements: "I am the light" (8:12); "I am the door" (10:9); "I am the resurrection and the life" (11:25); "I am the way, and the truth, and the life" (14:6). At other times, even more strangely, He identifies Himself with this very verb, *to be*, as if he were to say, "I am what it means to be'" which, in fact, He said: "I tell you the solemn truth, before Abraham came to be, *I am!*" (8:55). And in one, singular and extraordinary case this happens (I am reading from chapter 18 of the Gospel of John, the scene of Jesus' arrest):

> When he had finished praying, Jesus left with his disciples and crossed the Kidron Valley. On the other side there was a garden, and he and his disciples went into it. Now Judas, who betrayed him, knew the place, because Jesus had often met there with his disciples. So Judas came to the garden, guiding a detachment of soldiers and some officials from the chief priests and the Pharisees. They were carrying torches, lanterns and weapons. Jesus, knowing all that was going to happen to him, went out and asked them, "Who is it you want?" "Jesus of Nazareth," they replied. "I am," Jesus said. When Jesus said, "I am" they drew back and fell to the ground.

Julian gave an astute answer to the problem of the inconsistencies between the two Testaments that make up the Christian Bible by observing that inconsistency is all one should expect from a God who manifested himself as a Will and not as (more in line with classical rationalism) Reason. Will is a personal characteristic; we don't ascribed volition to impersonal forces and powers. And yet this is the fundamental mystery of God, that the power that creates and sustains everything, Life itself, wills that which He makes alive and brings to being—in fact, it is willing that brings it into existence. Your very existence is the proof of God's love for you.

11. That God *Is*

It is ridiculous to attempt to know God objectively, through such properties as substance, quantity, quality, etc., for then you are looking for an object; but this does not mean that God becomes reduced to subjective feeling, to a hope, to empty belief—"for its reality was presupposed in all the various manifestations of conscious life, of speculative as well as practical activity."[68] You cannot demonstrate gravity objectively—for which science has only a description but not an explanation— let alone such occult-like realities as dark matter (upon which science relies in order to explain some ninety percent of the universe)—itself, by definition, dark because unknown and perhaps even unknowable—*yet known by its effects*. So, one could easily argue, is God known, *by His effects*. The science of the spiritual world is as exact as that of the physical and its laws equally reliable. And in this sense God is the protagonist of the *Confessions*, as He is much of History, for He is an actor who is known through His effects and as the ultimate reason and cause of those effects.

The world is not a self-generating chaos because it can be known. Since it can be known—that is, since there is the possibility of science—it is *ordered*. You can phrase this argument differently: If there is science, then there is a creator God. The world, as we know it, is known, i.e.,

---

68 Charles Norris Cochrane, *Christianity and Classical Culture*, p. 401.

capable of being known and, with respect to ourselves and other animals, capable of knowing itself. Things in the world are defined; this, then, is a world that cannot be infinite. It is a defined world, and because it is defined, it must be created, for it is defined first and foremost by time, insofar as it has an absolute beginning prior to which it did not exist. It was brought into being at a moment in time (or better yet, at the moment that time begins). It could not have brought itself into existence because if it could have, it would have always already done so; but it didn't, so it can't. The world was brought into existence by something else, "which is what we all understand by God" (as St. Thomas says at the end of each of his Five Ways).

That the world exists demonstrates that something other than the world itself exists which is causally responsible for its existence. It is, therefore, possible to move on and venture a demonstration into what kind of being that Being who is responsible for our world is by looking at what kind of world it is, though perhaps a better path might be to think about what kind of being is the Being that would create in the first place. That is, the very fact that this Being makes something other than itself must say something about it: yes, it is a creating force, but what *generates* or what *motivates* its creative power?

It is a big, awesome world, of course. And you are now thinking of pictures that NASA has provided that depict the vast dark expanses of space and distant galaxies. But before you go there, pay attention to this little garden that is our planet. What does this garden say about its gardener? Let yourself first be awestruck by how that awesome creative power demonstrates itself through the frail petals of the phlox and the evanescence of its fragrance. He *preferred* that you know His power first as it is disguised behind the flowers (this is the demonstration based on Sherlock Holmes' "Sermon on the Rose")—and by that, you can know more about Him than any logical demonstrations. For He did not "expose the foundations of the world" (Ps. 18) to you. Science did so. Before science—driven, as it is, by the same curiosity of a child who breaks his toy in order to see what hides inside (see my "Radio Analogy" above)—tore the veil of teleological beauty asunder in order to expose the vast cosmic machines (all the more terrifying in their eternal silence) that operate behind the veil of our world's stage, God gave himself to us in flowers.

Every rose is a promise of eternity. Even though they themselves wither, still, flowers promise us eternity. Quoth the detective:

> "There is nothing in which deduction is so necessary as in religion," said he, leaning with his back against the shutters. "It can be built up as an exact science by the reasoner. Our highest assurance of the goodness of Providence seems to me to rest in the flowers. All other things, our powers, our desires, our food, are all really necessary for our existence in the first instance. But this rose is an extra. Its smell and its colour are an embellishment of life, not a condition of it. It is only goodness which gives extras, and so I say again that we have much to hope from the flowers."

Nature is scripture in the Scriptures: Within the Scriptures God uses nature (e.g., Elijah's raven, Jonah's vine) to reveal something about Himself. Even the parables of the New Testament with all the birds and vines and seeds are not merely didactic but apocalyptic. Didactic only to the extent that they teach us how to read the revelatory subtext in the script of creation. Apocalyptic (i.e., revelatory) in that they show us God's goodness.

12. The Doctrine of the Three Births

Each one of us has three births or becomings:

The first is when we are conceived; this is coming from nothing into being (something), being or becoming an embryo. This is our first stage of existence, when we are simply in a state of *being*. What is interesting here is that we build organs and develop capacities that are entirely impractical and impossible for this stage: lungs for breathing, for example. What could lungs mean to an embryo? Could an embryo even be made aware of them? Our sole purpose at this stage is to build a body for ourselves that will allow us to live in the world—but please note, a world of which we, as yet, know nothing. Suppose we had the ability to speak to a fetus, perhaps to console him as the time to be delivered approaches, and he feels, as he must, that he is being taken away from the only world he has known, that of his mother's warm and safe womb—suppose that we could speak to that fetus and try to explain to him that what he experiences as an end is only a beginning, a second birth and second becoming, this time from being to well-being, for this is a bigger, better world than his mother's womb, not only in space but in the incomparable richness of the experiences it affords us. He would neither believe us nor understand what we were saying.

We are like this embryo in this, the second stage of our existence—the stage of well-being in which we are not merely biological but also biographical beings. And we are like this embryo when we fail to believe and to understand any murmurs of another world; for the existence of a third birth into a third world would render life in this world not a place of destination but itineration.

But such third world does exist, because being and well-being are ultimately only *conditions* of ever-well-being. For well-being is not really *well*, that is good, if its goodness can be taken away, insofar as something given only for a period of time, however short or long, is not a gift but merely a loan (and we thus return full circle to Anaximander's ontological *mortgage*). No being is worth having if it be not good. As much as it is evident, therefore, that well-being presupposes being, it must be equally necessary that both exist for the sake of the ultimate good and the ultimate being, namely, the state of ever-well-being. I cannot be certain but I believe that it is sensible to expect that all the points of comparison between the first two states of human existence—that of the human embryo and the human being, that is, the unborn and born human being—apply also to a comparison between the second and the third: We can expect that in this world we build organs and develop capacities that, were we to be made fully aware of them, would be considered entirely impractical and impossible for this stage; we can expect that, as our purpose in that first state was to build a body that would allow us to live in this world, so is our purpose in this world, to prepare a body of some sort ("a spiritual body," St. Paul calls it) that would allow us to live in the world of ever-well-being; and we can expect that this third world is "bigger" and better than the second, in which we still live, as the second was by comparison to the first and that, therefore, wishing to remain in this world is as foolish as the wish of the embryo who would rather avoid being born.

When one begins to realize that there will be a time when you have left your house for the last time without knowing it or have performed any of those small mundane things that make up our everydayness *for the last time*—sure this thought oppresses us. But it is mere sentimentality based on our nearsightedness, forgetting, as you do, that not even for one day, not even for a moment in your life (in fact, the thought has never crossed your mind until now) have you regretted leaving behind your mother's womb.[69] On which basis, I expect that no one in the third stage of our existence will miss all the things we did "for the last time" in this life, for then it should be clear that to call it "last" was not true, and that the things left behind, the things that we now assume we will miss, will be surpassed by the things there, as much as life in the world surpasses life in the womb. In short, prepare to live forever!

But not in this intermediary state. Look around you. Everything you see is "going." No matter how big or how small: This wall here is "going," which means it has no permanence. The house, the city, the planet are sooner or later passing away. Some things will outlast us for a little while, others for much longer (by our estimates of counting time), but eventually they too shall pass away. The "passing" of the things of our world is not so much a characteristic that they have by themselves as it is the maker's mark of the world in this second stage of existence that we currently find ourselves. It is, as you would notice, a stage between the Alpha (being) and the

---

69   And yet—and this is the great paradox—man all his life is acting as if seeking nothing else than a return to his mother's womb. The *fallen* man, I should clarify. The most visible example is, of course, sex during which a man is trying, and failing, repeatedly to re-enter the same birth canal that gave birth to him. But the Oedipus complex (to speak Freudianese) is only the result of that which is Beyond the Pleasure Principle, namely the death drive. It is not entirely honest, however: Man enjoys re-enacting this return to nothingness knowing very well that it is only a momentary suspension of existence, after which he will return to himself and return to the economy of his political life (see, Aristophanes' speech in Plato's *Symposium*): relieved and refreshed. His death in bed was only a play—it would have been an entirely different story were man to really die immediately after orgasm.

Omega (ever-well-being). It is in its *character*, therefore, to be passing and, as result, everything that finds itself in it passes away as well. It makes, therefore, no sense to desire to stay here forever.

13. Through Fire and Water

Beauchard must have found the doctrine of the three births quite captivating for, carried away no doubt by my masterful oration, and mesmerized by the promise that my little theory held for us all, he did the incomprehensible. With his right hand reached inside the breast pocket of his jacket and . . .

"He pulled a gun?!"

No, not a gun, dear Reader, but something far worse. He took a smokebox from his jacket pocket, one embossed with an S on the face of it and pulled from it something between a cigar and a cigarette, a cigarillo, one of those that had been dipped in cognac, an Al Capone *if memory serves, which is now impossible to find anywhere in Massachusetts.*

"Where did he find those?" *I thought.*

Unfortunately, it was just then that Burnop stood up and started protesting and making snide comments about the smell of smoke. Beauchard extinguished the cigarillo and we all tried to return our focus to the lecture at hand, but Burnop persisted in his whines, screeching, "It stinks!"

Beauchard offered to open a window to let some air into the room and, indeed, in no less than five minutes the air in the room had become fresh and cool. But Burnop wouldn't drop it. He kept shaking his hand in front of his nose theatrically as if he was trying to clear the lingering smell of smoke.

"The stench!" *he exhaled.*

"I perceive that it is not the smoke that is your problem," *said Beauchard calmly*, "but the smoker. You want to punish me for smoking in a classroom against the rules of propriety; no, the smoke is not the problem, for it has already been addressed, but you can't give it a rest until you have extracted your pound of flesh by humiliating me. But I see your sadism," *he added,* "and I call it for what it is."

During the ensuing altercation, the cigarillo, which we believed to have been extinguished, was slowly setting the wastebin on fire. The smoke—if not the very temperature of the people in the room, rising with all screaming and shouting—activated the sprinklers which drenched everyone in the seminar room with a sobering dose of water, thus bringing my lecture to its inglorious conclusion.

Back in the cold night, I found myself walking through the dark campus with President Jospeh. I tried to say something about what had happened by quoting a line from the Psalms ("We went through fire and through water") *but he wasn't in the mood for chitchat.*

"Let me get myself out of these wet clothes and into a dry martini" *he murmured.*

Just then, I noticed a severely bloated thirty-something in sweatpants and a hoodie. He was a boyish manchild who looked like he could have been a young Fenwickian, if not for his advanced age. He hurried past us rudely, nearly spilling his iced coffee on the sidewalk in front of him.

"What's wrong with that young loafer?" *I asked the President, pointing to the slovenly chud, an insolent flaneur who went around thinking that his opinions were the only ones that mattered.*

"Him?" *the President said,* "I am afraid that, for better or worse, he is our future."

Epilogue

This was the last time Father Manoussakis spoke in public. His visit to Fenwick University became his last appearance. After giving the Fenwick Lectures, Manoussakis withdrew entirely from the world and, as if obeying an omen or expiating a crime, he became a silent recluse for the rest of his life. There is no record, not even a picture, of him after 2020—a stark contrast with the earlier years that were frivolously well-documented down to the minutest detail. As a result, very little is known about the years he spent in seclusion until his death. They say that toward the end of his life, he received the company of only a handful of friends, although the names that have surfaced—a Hutch Beechcraft, an Oliver Crayphius, a certain Dora of no other known qualities, and the man who calls himself Stesichorus—sound spurious and, frankly, ridiculous. This has given rise to the equally farcical theory that even the few friends who are said to have paid him the occasional visit during those years of his voluntary seclusion were, in truth, but *one* friend, single and singular, who took it upon himself to play all those fanciful parts and don all those improbable names as *masks* in order to entertain his lonely old friend. A solitary theater made up of many roles but with only one actor and one lone spectator. If this was the case with Fr. Manoussakis, thankfully it is not so with these Lectures, his last public word (for everything else published after

them should be considered a posthumous publication),
which have gained a surprising notoriety among discerning bibliophiles around the world and have become the
inspiration for generations of young philosophers.

Louis Light
Master of the Vault and Keeper of Secrets
Fenwick University

Appendix

Autograph notes of *The Fenwick Lectures*

(from the Fenwick Archives, folio 6729/19)

On the Human Being:

The human being is a <u>position</u> and a <u>look</u>.

The Greek word for Man – in the broad sense of the human being — is "ἄνθρωπος, (a word that you might recognise in such derivatives as ~~its epigone~~ "anthropology"); but ἄνθρωπος, unlike the Latin word for human and humanity which names Man's origins, speaks of Man's destiny — or Man's sin.

(*) "Ἄνθρωπος means looking-up (ἄνω θρώσκω): here you have a position (up) and a look: a look that is directed up-wards. "Upwards" is relative to the speaker's position (or the subject's position), the subject which is looking up, by understanding and speaking of the direction of his look as up (higher) in relation to himself, who must, therefore, be lower, he must be down. I don't think you can look up unless you are down. <u>Anthropos</u> then presupposes and indicates the human: that is the being who came from earth (<u>humus</u>). It is the "same" word — or the same meaning and understanding — with the word Adam, from the Hebrew <u>adamah</u> (the ground, earth). The human being is the <u>earthly</u> being, with everything that that means.

"Ἄνθρωπος means the earthly being has risen up, it has emerged from its ground and can now stand up and walk, instead of crawl, (although it still crawls until it learns how to walk — for each one of us in our individual lives repeat and rehearse the evolution of our species —) and because it can now stand up and walk can now see, it now has the look (even though it has to loose, the <u>smell</u>, which is taste, that is, the ability of <u>sapio</u>, the ability of <u>sapere</u>, that is of savouring, of tasting and of being sorry — for <u>homo sapiens</u> can be sapient only as long as he remains close to the ground — homo > humus); now he stands up, his <u>eyes</u>, <u>not</u> his mouth and his nose are the discerning instruments — eyes and ears, the senses of distance and distant (of Knowledge as <u>distance</u> and as <u>difference</u>); mouth and nose, the senses of proximity and intimacy — that's a different kind of knowledge than the knowledge of the eyes that is almost entirely lost to us.

anthropoid,
anthropophagy,
lycanthropy, epicanthropy, and
anthropomorphism. —

anthropoid,
anthropophagy,

On the Human Being:

On the Soul (2)

if ...

The Illusion of Identity: ④

I will now discuss a little further these two points that our inquiry has discovered ... under I have stated them. So that.

The Illusion of Identity: ③

|| For I don't do that which I want but that which I don't want — that I do. ||

The illusion of identity: ②

The expression that I have used just now it will become significant much later but if you look carefully at it you might be able to see that hints upon the mystery of time — what is time? — and the fact that in consciousness — for consciousness is this splitting of ourselves in time that makes, produces, excretes time.

But I have to first explain this splitting, consciousness from where we see it operating (and operating as a duality) within concrete — everyday — experience For this splitting makes itself known [con-science] as division [con-sciousness]

The notion of identity: ①

as in cases when we judge someone as acting "out of character" (or speaking): I couldn't imagine he did it or he could do such a thing, says the neighbor of a serial killer. Characters in history and books have been dismissed from saying or doing something because they had made a different claim earlier, etc. All such occasions and modes of thinking presuppose about us something that is not evident, or evidently given in our experience, namely a permanence (an unchangeable) over time that is characterized by constancy and unity of thought and action. That we are not. We are, instead, notoriously mutable influence of our feelings and thoughts under the ... of our instincts, suggestible ... weather. We are much more anatomically, we are ... tion and border between ... ated by "space", permeated, outside it. ... many. The lack of identity ... entity, namely constancy, continuously make ... à la Sartre, not to decide is ... or rather ... other ways ... of a multiplicity in us. ... we are faced with a delusion ... itself had split into two

Your sword — that is, yourself — has been broken into pieces. Until you [forge and] weld those pieces together again and out of them forge a whole one sword, you will be impotent against all your enemies, without your sword you are weak.

Allow me to continue with some other illustrations – parables they are called — while I leave music aside for the moment:

① The Parable of the Rich Fool (Luke 12: 16-21)

"And I will say to my soul, Soul, thou hast much goods laid up for many years;
[you may have the many goods but do you have the many years?]
Take thine ease, eat, drink, and be merry.
But God said unto him, Thou Fool, this night thy soul shall be required of thee, then whose shall those things be, which thou hast provide? "

body (and you are so proud that it is "your my right" you say) well, not even this body is properly your property you will leave it behind — a handfull of dust and a few bones so it can be given to others.'

I cannot pursue any further the question of property here but I promise to return to it later (Cephalus will remind us of it). I return to death to say that, even though, it might be considered an adrene to our life, it, nevertheless, disabuse us from holding the false notion that life belongs to us.

" Thou Fool, this night thy soul shall be required of thee " How can it be "required" of him, (that is, taken away from him —and can you imagine something worse but also more just that it can happen to a rich man their taking away not what he has but that by which he can enjoy what he has?) unless it wasn't his to begin with? You are not life however but alive, you have life and you have it, as Anaximander suggests, on loan. A loan to be paid back in full with death. A mortage.

Anaximander's fragment is one of the earliest utterances of philosophy and unexpectedly dark for a saying of a Greek. It says that everything that exists and insofar as, by existing, it is a being and not the Being, anything that has being or existence but cannot claim to be life or existence has committed a terrible crime for which they must atone, or rather they must be punished by returning to the same nothingness from which they emerged when the came-to-be (because) And it is the very possibility of their punishment, of our punishment, for I speak of ourselves as well, it is the very possibility of their punishment that is the proof of their own guilt and crime. That life can and will be taken away from us is the proof that it wasn't ours to have it to begin wit But we do have it and that can only mean that we stole it.

Earth, soil, dust : a civilization of death

Sisyphus : the most human of man; the man closest to earth
the man who has eaten most dust
a successful man according to Homer (ὁ κέρδιστος γένετ᾽ ἀνδρῶν
Iliad VI, 153)

μὴ ἐλπίζετε ἐπὶ ἀδικίαν
καὶ ἐπὶ ἅρπαγμα μὴ ἐπιποθεῖτε,
πλοῦτος ἐὰν ῥέῃ, μὴ προστίθεσθε καρδίαν
Ps. 61/62: 11

The Magic Mountain
takes place in a sanatorium, a place that is a cross between a hotel and a hospital
it resembles, by inversion, like a reflection, Book XI of the Odyssey, where Odysseus
in order to return home, to his life (to his wife and kingdom, his Ithaca), must first
descend to Hades. He must, that is, undergo a symbolic death, so that the much-
desired and sought-after return to Ithaca can only be achieved posthumously.
[Canto I by Ezra Pound is a poetic translation of Odyssey's XI' (Νέκυια, Nekyia)

The Magic Mountain is such a Nekyia — in both senses of a necromancy
and a Katabasis. It includes two terrifying scenes / episodes of necromancy
(ch. 7, but another one earlier?) and it is itself a Katabasis in reverse (see, p. 66 "satanic" ch. 3,
the hero's dialogue with Herr Settembrini). Comparison with the way down (and the way up
in Plato's Republic .

The Value of Wealth:

Value: valorem (valor), valere: to be well, strong (ὑγιαίνω)

    strong in life: valiant (for a human)

    strong for life: valuable (for a thing)

                                                    or availing

Ruskin: „To be 'valuable', therefore, is 'to avail towards life'. A truly valuable thing is that which leads to life with its whole strength" (Ad Valorem, p 95)

Wealth:

[Ruskin quoting Mill] "To be wealthy is to have a large stock of useful articles".

To have [the meaning of Possession]:

The relic of a Saint (in the Cathedral of Milano) holds a golden staff and wears an emerald cross — does it have them? (In what sense can be said that the relic „has" the possession of the gold and the emeralds?) [Ad Val. p 101]

And, if wealth is defined as "having a large stock of useful things, it is implied in fact assumed in that „usefully that is the use of a thing that makes which makes you it useful and worth having it and capable of having it, for you have it, only as long as you can use it. Possession is determined by the ability which to use, so that one cannot use, one does not, strictly speaking, have and — if he has it beyond its use then he abuses it. (If he is not using it, he is abusing it, for having it and keeping it — preventing it from being used. To prevent the use of the useful is to abuse it. *⊗

    Wealth, then, should serve health — that is, making one whole. (here also in the sense of not lacking) thus full but full to capacity, so to speak, because if you keep adding beyond the point capacity you don't add value (make it stronger) but you make it weaker, you weaken it as if you keep feeding a body beyond what it needs you don't strengthen it but that very thing that strengthened it, namely food, weakens it and makes it sick, ill. Similarly, all wealth that is beyond one's capacity to use it does not make him wealthier but illthier.

Μελέτη Θανάτου 2

With the advent of technology, however and especially bio-technology, and the A.I. and so on, some people, embolded by their advances, have ~~began~~ flirting, and I'm afraid, in earnest, with the idea of a man-made deathlessness. Man wants (again) to become immortal. There are some wealthy men — see that already since the Parable of the Rich Fool (Luke 12:16-21) death has been the worst nightmare of the rich, for it robs them from what they value most: not their life, but their wealth. By examining the urgency with which ~~a rich person~~ the wealthy are currently w employing every mean available to them to eradicate death you can understand the power, the fear, that death has over a mind sick with greed, for he, death alone, can show and will show with certainty how meaningless their possessions are for, as I'll explain later on, they don't actually possess them — and they know it — for man can possess only what he uses and only for as long as he uses it." ~~know that~~ The innovation that you are about to see being put into the pursuit ~~Technological achievement~~ of immortality is not motivated by philanthropy, or the passion for expanding our scientific horizons, for it is not ~~motivated~~ aiming at the continuation of life but at the continuation of possession, that is, of guaranteeing that one will continue to enjoy what he has for ~~as~~ ever.

But — to return to my point — granted that such immortality has been achieved, the question remains: is a deathless life livable? If by "deathless" you think "a little longer" of course, and with pleasure, but "deathless" means something more: it means endless. And endless is a very long time! Would you get married, for example, in such a deathless life, knowing, realizing, after the first 100, 200 years, or let's be generous in our calculations, after a few centuries of marriage to your lovely — and, sadly, equally deathless — spouse that you will be together, not "till death do us part", as you said at your wedding but for ever, — not realising that you could make that promise, and you could make the commitment that follows from that promise that was, precisely because death was to do you part? And, following this example, wouldn't any other action that requires a commitment on our part, a commitment of our time, become similarly impossible in a deathless existence? Why undertake learning a language today if you will be around for ever? There is no urgency, no need attached to this today anymore. You can do it tomorrow or in a hundred years from now — what difference does it make?

Μελέτη θανάτου 3

⊛ That is, I don't use these terms — life and death — absolutely, but as conditioned by human existence in the world

It makes no difference, for there is no difference between life and death.

[Here a caveat is necessary: I don't suggest that death is one pole of a dialectical opposition between life and death and that, without death life would have been meaningless.⊛ What I'm trying to say that for us, such as we are, *mortals*, destined to die there is no other point of departure for beginning to make sense of what it means to be a human being than by taking into account ~~that~~ these certainties, these facts that make our facticity — the facts that make us :

① you will die and ~~that human life is not endless, but it ends (again: this is in respect to human experience in this world)~~

② you don't know when — it could be at any time ~~that one cannot know with any certainty the hour of his death~~

These two seem to be the most basic rules or conditions of this game that we call life. If it is so, and I can't see how it might be other, then it is <u>essential</u> that you know them and take them continuously into your consideration, if you are to play well, that is, if you are to <u>live well</u>.

Let me repeat this and remember how we began this inquiry into Plato's (S's) understanding of philosophy in the <u>Phaedo</u> as μελέτη θανάτου — I repeat then, that if you want to live well you must always remember these two rules of life: that you will die and that you don't, cannot, know when.

You see, it wouldn't be fair to discuss health or wealth, pleasures or pains, without taking these two facts into consideration. It wouldn't, for example, be good to consider how good is to have a lot of goods, unless you knew and you remember that there are to no good to you beyond the grave, and that therefore, their value is relative to the use that they can be put-in in this life. And the same relative character must be assigned not only to wealth but also to health, and to knowledge, and to science, and to everything else. You should <u>evaluate</u> every thing by asking how does it stand with respect to death. Will it withstand death or will it be useful in teaching you how to die? For to live well must ultimately mean knowing how to die — knowing, first of all, how to deal with the certainty, with the facticity of your death. For one lives badly when they don't know how to die. If you are pretending that you don't, for example.

(✳) Because if you do that and you are able to be happy in it, you may discover that you don't have to conquer it, you don't have to possess it, and that will save you a lot of trouble (and maybe a little bit of money). –

Value of Wealth

In your age money has a particular value insofar as it guarantees a certain degree of <u>independence</u>.
It is not so much a question of simply having money, but of having you <u>own money</u>. Fair enough.

But, what about one's <u>dependance</u> on money, the very money, ironically, with which you buy your independance? You have simply exchanged masters. Before you were depedant on those who provided you with money, now you are depedant on money (you call them "your own" but, believe me, they have passed through many other hands) and, ultimately, on those who "make" them for you (no one really makes money — no-one can; you can only make things or provide services that you sell for money) — your employer or your customers.
Free (from money; not "free to make money" whichever way is faster and most profitable), free, that is, truly independent is he who does not need money and who can provide for his needs himself with the labor of his hands or his mind. Free, once again, is he who <u>needs</u> less, not he who has (because he needs) <u>more</u>.

(<u>Death in the City</u>, 3:)

We meet here one of the earliest collective unconsciouns, memories of the so to speak, of humanity: a memory, the memory of a primordial crime and of an ancient, ancestral guilt — the memory of a sin that is <u>original</u>, that is, contemporaneous to the origins of our human race and perhaps that is the sin, as Anaximander articulated in his own language, to have an origin, to have <u>originated</u>. That Man had always — certainly <u>before</u> his historical existence, pretentions to existence and sought to usurp it for himself has been amply testified by the literature of every ancient culture. In <u>Genesis</u> it is the promise of becoming like Gods " (3:5) that prompts the crime that brings about the punishment of our mortality. In other words, we die because we tried to be like gods. In the story of Prometheus the idea is similar: Prometheus — the hero who acts on behalf of the human race and to its benefit — <u>steals</u> the fire, that up to this point has belonged only to the gods, and gives it to humans (which allows them to survive that is, to live; it is easy to see here how fire is an image of civilization but also of life as sustained by civilization, <u>not</u> nature, that is; life as sustained by Man's himself). And his punishment is to be fixed on a rock — prefiguring the Sisyphean life of man who is tied on this rock that is our planet — and have his liver — a vital organ, representing one's vitality — eaten daily by an eagle.

There is much to be said on Anaximander's dark saying — especially, what makes the difference between life been considered, in his view, a crime, and life been consider, in our view, a gift — but there is only one more feature of this saying that interests us in our present inquiry. This <u>cycle</u> of comings, be- coming to being, and return from non-being to being and returning back to non-being lurks somewhere behind another idea that some of you might be familiar with, namely the idea of <u>reincarnation</u> or <u>metapsychosis</u> which is debated for the first time on the last day of Socrates' life in the Plato's dialogue, the <u>Phaedo</u> (70c–72e). The idea of reincarnation is, in essence, a theory of maintaining <u>equilibrium</u> between living and death by a continuous process of <u>recycling</u> that provides for the continuation of all things and of the human race. Your grandfather dies but your grandson is born. What exactly <u>is</u> recycled is not immediately clear. Traditionally it is thought that the souls are recycled but this must be even more the case for matter, thus making this theory the forerunner, in some oblique way, of the <u>principle of mass conservation</u> (Lavoisier)

There is an <u>economy</u> of both matter and spirit whose regulation has always been assumed by the <u>City</u> (by the <u>Polis</u>) that gives a <u>political</u> dimension to death.

On the Human Being ③ :

And good sense of smell can help an animal "see" farther than human eyes can see, and I mean farther into the past and [further] into the future — for it is by smell that a dog can sense the onset of a disease as yet undiagnosed and undetected, and can tell who has been in a room hours [or even days] ago when you can only see what is in front of the eyes at present. Or, to put it better, if Man in his epistemology is unable to move beyond the present, is because he can believe only what he sees but he can only see what is presented to him, that is, only the present. Smell, and taste, on the other hand, can give much more efficient and effective access to the past — as the famous episode of the little madeleines in Proust's In Search of Lost Time:

"...one day in winter, on my return home, my mother, seeing that I was cold, offered me some tea, a thing I did not ordinary take. I declined at first, and then, for no particular reason, changed my mind. (...) And soon, mechanically, dispirited after a dreary day with the prospect of a depressing morrow, I raised to my lips a spoonful of the tea in which I had soaked a morsel of the cake. No sooner had the warm liquid mixed with the crumbs touched my palate than a shiver ran through me, and I stopped, intent upon the extraordinary thing that was happening to me." (Swann's Way, p. 45)

What follows is nothing less than a quasi-religious conversion, a mystical experience of smell and taste:

"An exquisite pleasure had invaded my senses, something isolated, detached, with no suggestion of its origin. And at once the vicissitudes of life had become indifferent to me, its disasters innocuous, its brevity illusory — the new sensation having had the effect, which love has, of filling me with a precious essence; or rather this essence was not in me, it was me. I had ceased to feel mediocre, contingent, mortal. Whence could it have come to me, this all-powerful joy?" (Ibid.)

The remaining seven volumes of this novel is the answer to this very question. What interests us in the present discussion is that it is a joy that is not intellectual or cerebral, it is not a vision but a taste, a foretaste, if you prefer, of an eschatological happiness, for it defies the death that engulfs history and is history in the endless accumulation of yesterdays. Here the past is not lost and time is regained:

"...when from a long-distant past nothing subsists, after the people are dead, after the things are broken and scattered, taste and smell alone, more fragile but more enduring, more immaterial, more persistent, more faithful, remain poised a long time, like souls, remembering, waiting, hoping,

Disclosure

(To the Reader)

The subject-matter of these lectures are the fundamental concepts and structures (language, technology, civilization, humanity) of this world that is passing. There will come a day, sooner or later, when the *scheme* of this world (to use St. Paul's expression—Heidegger would have said *Gestell*) will be no more, and on that they, they will become completely irrelevant. Until then, however, they will prove an immense benefit for whomsoever cares to study them. Should God wish to preserve them in whatever form or mode He deems appropriate in all eternity (insofar as they contain something of His words, which shall never pass), the author of these lectures makes no objections, and he shall remain, as in everything else, eternally grateful.

www.ingramcontent.com/pod-product-compliance
Lightning Source LLC
Chambersburg PA
CBHW030933060726
47591CB00005B/1783